THE STRUGGLES OF RECOVERING ASSETS FOR HOLOCAUST SURVIVORS

JOINT HEARING

BEFORE THE

SUBCOMMITTEE ON
THE MIDDLE EAST AND NORTH AFRICA

AND THE

SUBCOMMITTEE ON EUROPE, EURASIA, AND
EMERGING THREATS

OF THE

COMMITTEE ON FOREIGN AFFAIRS
HOUSE OF REPRESENTATIVES

ONE HUNDRED THIRTEENTH CONGRESS

SECOND SESSION

_____

SEPTEMBER 18, 2014

_____

Serial No. 113–210

_____

Printed for the use of the Committee on Foreign Affairs

Available via the World Wide Web: http://www.foreignaffairs.house.gov/ or
http://www.gpo.gov/fdsys/

_____

U.S. GOVERNMENT PRINTING OFFICE

89–815PDF   WASHINGTON : 2014

_____

For sale by the Superintendent of Documents, U.S. Government Printing Office
Internet: bookstore.gpo.gov   Phone: toll free (866) 512–1800; DC area (202) 512–1800
Fax: (202) 512–2104   Mail: Stop IDCC, Washington, DC 20402–0001

CONTENTS

THE STRUGGLES OF RECOVERING ASSETS FOR HOLOCAUST SURVIVORS

THURSDAY, SEPTEMBER 18, 2014

House of Representatives,
Subcommittee on the Middle East and North Africa and
Subcommittee on Europe, Eurasia, and Emerging Threats,
Committee on Foreign Affairs,
Washington, DC.

The subcommittee met, pursuant to notice, at 3:05 p.m., in room 2172, Rayburn House Office Building, Hon. Ileana Ros-Lehtinen (chairman of the subcommittee) presiding.

Ms. Ros-Lehtinen. The joint subcommittee will come to order.

After recognizing myself, Chairman Rohrabacher, Ranking Member Deutch, Ranking Member Keating for opening statements, we will then recognize other members seeking recognition and we will hear from our witnesses.

Without objection, the witnesses' prepared statements will be made a part of the record and members may have 5 days in which to insert statements and questions for the record, subject to the length limitation in the rules.

The Chair now recognizes herself for 5 minutes.

This is a hearing we never should have to hold. Yet, it is a topic that must be addressed as Holocaust survivors around the world continue to suffer injustices of the past and their needs and well-being go neglected.

I want to acknowledge our late Congressman, the chairman of this committee, Tom Lantos, whose painting adorns the wall, a Holocaust survivor with whom I worked closely during his time here on the committee.

Six million Jews were murdered at the hands of the Nazis during the Holocaust, and millions more suffered unspeakable atrocities committed against them and their loved ones. All of their properties and belongings were stolen as the Nazis deported them to ghettos and concentration camps where most of them died of starvation, exhaustion, torture, or in gas chambers.

The toll the Holocaust has taken on survivors is unimaginable and it is unforgivable, but we cannot forget that it takes a tremendous toll on the second generation as well, as we will hear from our brave witnesses.

Today there are less than ½ million survivors of humanity's darkest period, with nearly half of all survivors worldwide living at or below the poverty level, and it is painful to see those who have suffered so greatly continue to struggle day in and day out as if they had not suffered enough.

And with the average age of Holocaust survivors estimated at 82, time is truly running out for us to bring them some sort of justice, some kind of closure, so that they can live out the rest of their lives in dignity and comfort.

I believe that more can and must be done. Holocaust survivors are barred from suing in Federal courts those insurance companies that failed to pay out Holocaust-era policies. At the very minimum, given that no money can ever replace the experience of suffering under the Nazis—at the very minimum, we should let the survivors and their families have their day in court.

Another avenue for the survivors was the International Commission on Holocaust Era Insurance Claims, ICHEIC, which closed in 2007, no matter how many times they say it is never closed. This system was flawed due to the problems with accountability and oversight, which led to—listen to this—84 percent of the claims being rejected, 84 percent being rejected.

These survivors and their families need to be made whole, and this is why it is vital for Germany and other nations to fulfill their obligations and for insurance companies that have been running out the clock in a deliberate attempt to avoid paying out rightful claims to be held accountable and to finally pay for what they owe these survivors, for what they owe these survivors.

These countries and these greedy insurance companies owe these survivors. This is what is rightfully theirs and what has been denied to them for decades, forcing them to relive this atrocity over and over again.

And it is not just these insurance companies and foreign governments that have let our Holocaust survivors down. We need to take a closer look at what more our own Government, the United States Government, can be doing as well.

As a Member of Congress who represents Holocaust survivors, I hear from my constituents that we in Congress must do more. Folks like Joe Sachs, like David Mermelstein, folks we will hear from today, they tell me that all the time.

I have heard repeatedly concerns from some of my constituents regarding the failure, the deception, the lies of the Claims Conference and how, though this is intended to help survivors receive fair compensation, it has been an impediment in the process.

Just like so many other senior citizens, survivors need extensive medical care. They are likely to have greater health needs than the general population and are more likely to face a number of certain illnesses, such as chronic depression, cognitive impairments, osteoporosis, post-traumatic stress syndrome. It is, therefore, vital for survivors to receive the financial, medical, and social support that so many desperately need.

Struggling to make ends meet and still fighting to correct the injustices of the past, it is important to hear from Holocaust survivors and their relatives as they share their stories and their daily struggles that they face as they seek to live out the remainders of their lives in security and dignity. Is that too much to ask?

ICHEIC has let Holocaust survivors down, no matter how the members of ICHEIC spin this. So it is up to us in Congress to step up and help the survivors.

Thank you.

And I am looking forward to hearing from our witnesses.

And I would like to point out that we have a person in the audience who is very interested in this—I am sorry if I don't pronounce your name correctly—Yael Fuchs, who is the Assistant Attorney General, Charities Bureau of the State of New York, Office of the Attorney General. Thank you very much.

And they have been closely following the plight of survivors and want to see justice for them.

And, with that, I turn to a fighter for Holocaust survivors and—from his early days as a college activist and even before, Congressman Ted Deutch.

Thank you, Ted.

Mr. DEUTCH. Madam Chairman, thank you. I want to thank you not for just calling today's hearing, but I want to thank you for being such a tremendous advocate and a partner in our efforts to ensure that every single survivor can live out their lives in dignity.

I want to recognize and I want to thank our witnesses for being here, in particular, my constituents from South Florida, Jack Rubin and Eugenie Lieberman.

Over the years, Jack has shared his own story and has shed light on the plight of other survivors so many times here in Congress, and he has done it out of his commitment to achieve justice.

And, Jack, I am grateful that you are here with us once again today.

I am privileged to represent a significant number of survivors in South Florida, like the chairman as well. I often speak of how, when I was first elected to office in 2006, it used to be standing room only at the Yom HaShoa at the Holocaust Remembrance Day events, and every year, unfortunately, there are more and more empty seats.

The survivor population, a group that endured some of the greatest horrors in history, is now one of our most vulnerable. Today we will examine the particularly unique set of challenges to and the needs of the survivor community.

According to most estimates, there are over 500,000 survivors worldwide with roughly 120,000 survivors living in the United States. Estimates show that up to half live in poverty.

Survivors face a set of challenges different from most older Americans. Their experiences have left them fearful of the loss of control and independence that can come with aging, and the thought of depending on meal services or institutionalized care can dredge up painful memories.

Most survivors are dependent on social service agencies to supplement their needs. However, for survivors, the process of applying for assistance or filing claims can be difficult and can be painful. Some are still wary of disclosing too much personal information. Often survivors may be unaware of what benefits and resources are available to them.

The Jewish family service agencies on the ground in our communities, other social service agencies who work with them, face the daunting task of allocating funds for survivor care that are, quite frankly, never enough.

According to the Association of Jewish Family and Children's agencies, an umbrella organization of social service providers, its members report that they require anywhere from an additional $100,000 to $4 million per year to provide for the basic needs of survivors in their communities.

Some communities have resorted to private fundraising to fill this gap, but most survivors do not want the American taxpayer to shoulder the cost of their care.

The Conference on Jewish Material Claims—the Claims Conference was established to negotiate reparations from the German Government, and it is worth remembering that German Chancellor Konrad Adenauer pledged to care for every survivor until their last breath.

Unfortunately, in recent years, the Claims Conference has been plagued by accusations of mismanagement of funds. And I was extremely concerned to see the recent announcement that the Claims Conference was going to consider devoting more and more of their resources to Holocaust education rather than to the care for survivors. I am glad to see that this decision has since been reversed.

I also remain concerned that there is not an updated accurate accounting of survivors' needs, and I welcome the recent steps taken to address this issue. This administration has also taken a series of steps to help survivors.

The State Department, under the leadership of the Special Envoy for Holocaust issues, has been intimately involved in pressing European capitals to pass restitution laws, but more must be done to ensure that those who have not enacted restitution laws do so and that those who have are actually abiding by these laws.

Under the leadership of Vice President Biden, the White House last year announced a new initiative to aid survivors, including the appointment of a special envoy for Holocaust survivor services that serves as a liaison between communities and social service agencies, a volunteer training program to build the capacity of these agencies, and $5 million in the President's budget to leverage a public-private partnership.

But despite the best intentions—the best-intentioned efforts to aid survivors, the unfortunate reality is that care is still lacking. These men and women who have overcome life's most unimaginable horrors should not live one more day in poverty.

Madam Chairman, the simple fact is that we cannot allow one more survivor to have to face the painful choice of whether to buy that month's medicine or groceries.

As the population ages, there are many survivors who will need round-the-clock care. Constraints placed on funding and caps on home-care hours prevent them from getting the care they desperately need while being able to remain in the comfort and familiarity of their own home.

Chairman Ros-Lehtinen and I have in past years introduced the Tom Lantos Justice for Holocaust Survivors Act, named for the former chairman of this committee, the only Holocaust survivor to serve in Congress.

Too often the process of filing claims for property or insurance policies was far too arduous for survivors and their heirs. Finding proper documentation left over after the war is nearly impossible. There must be a better way to ensure that these families get the justice that they deserve.

Madam Chairman, there are 500,000 survivors worldwide, a number that is decreasing every day. We must get an accurate understanding of the needs of the community, not the needs based on limitations imposed by existing agreements, but what it will actually cost to ensure that every survivor can live out his or her life in dignity, and we need to find the money to provide that care. That is what we owe our survivors.

I stand ready to help. I will work with the Claims Conference. I will work with local social service agencies, with the survivor community, with any group that wants to help.

But instead of fighting about the merits of particular actions that have been taken over the years, let's agree that at this point time is running out for the survivors, and let's figure out what's necessary to do and then let's get it done.

I can't—I can't adequately express my gratitude to the witnesses for being here today to courageously share their stories or the stories of their loved ones. Please know that we are committed to working until every survivor gets the care they need and until every survivor gets the respect that they deserve.

I yield back.

Ms. ROS-LEHTINEN. Thank you very much, Mr. Deutch.

And I am so pleased that Mr. Rohrabacher and Mr. Keating's subcommittee have joined in this effort to get justice for Holocaust survivors.

So I am pleased to yield to our subcommittee chair, Dana Rohrabacher of California.

Mr. ROHRABACHER. Thank you very much. And I would like to thank Chairwoman Ros-Lehtinen and Ranking Member Deutch for their great leadership on this issue.

My committee was invited to participate, and we are proud to participate today and to support you in this very worthwhile and admirable endeavor. So you can call on us, too. We again thank you for this. And I am pleased that we are able to hold this as a joint hearing today and that may make this a joint project.

This afternoon's hearing is on the struggle to recover the assets of Holocaust survivors and to consider their well-being. It is an important and timely subject, as we have already heard.

There are about 100,000 Holocaust survivors in the United States today. But due to the passage of time, that number is reduced nearly every day. Those survivors have been a living memorial to the tragedy and the crime of the Holocaust. It is a very good thing that today we are discussing how each one of them can find justice and compensation, even if it is delayed.

I understand that a large percentage of survivors live near the poverty line. Perhaps a quarter of them in the United States live below that threshold. And it is a very sad statistic. Yet, I am glad that there are Jewish organizations working to help alleviate the harsh conditions in which too many of these survivors live. These groups have my sincere thanks and my admiration.

Too often horrible things happen to innocent people in this world, but I am reminded of the saying, "The arc of the moral universe is long, but it bends toward justice." And I think that is clearly the case here. It says something about what we are going to hear about today.

And we have some heroic witnesses, including Holocaust—a Holocaust survivor and the family of two Holocaust survivors. And I thank them for being here and sharing their story with us, giving us a human face to the statistics that we can talk about. But it is really the human face that we are concerned about today.

After the end of a conflict or war, it is often impossible to return land or property to its former civilian owners in a timely fashion, even if at all. But what we should make sure that we strive to ensure is that there be an equitable compensation for victims in this situation.

During this hearing, I have learned more about the living conditions of Holocaust survivors and how we can make sure that their care and medical attention is there but, also, in how we bring justice to this issue.

Thank you again for holding the hearing. I am happy to have my committee as a part of this.

Ms. ROS-LEHTINEN. Thank you so much, Mr. Rohrabacher. We are blessed to have you join in this effort, and we thank you for that great opening remark.

And now we would like to turn to the ranking member of that subcommittee, Mr. Keating of Massachusetts.

Mr. KEATING. Thank you, Madam Chairman.

And I would like to thank our witnesses today, as their testimonies will allow us to determine the needs of Holocaust survivors in our communities and do everything to make sure those needs are met.

As a young boy growing up in Sharon, Massachusetts, one of my neighbors was a survivor of a concentration camp. I didn't understand everything I understand now. I recall seeing the tattooed—tattoos on her wrist and inquired as to what that was all about.

And as I reflect back now, being more mature and understanding more about what she went through, in growing up with her family and going to school with her children, I now can reflect fully on the challenges that she had. Sadly, she is now deceased. But estimates indicate that up to 5,000 survivors live in my home State of Massachusetts.

One organization called Schechter Holocaust Services currently provides services to approximately 200 of these survivors, which include emergency financial assistance, home-care services, and case management. Eighty-six percent of this organization's clients are over the age of 75, and 56 percent are female. Fifty-four percent have Russian as their primary language, which is why assistance is provided both in Russian and in English.

Since the tale of the survivors tell us so much more than statistics can ever do, Schechter Holocaust Services has graciously allowed me to share a story that illustrates the needs of this population.

Mrs. G is an 87-year-old woman. She was 8 years old when she was sent out of Germany alone to escape the Nazis. Her parents were killed. She settled in the Boston area and later married and had one child, who developed severe mental illness as a teen. Mr. G died 20 years ago and, since then, Mrs. G has struggled to provide for herself and to provide for her daughter, who is now 65 years old.

Mrs. G was introduced to Schechter Holocaust Services and was able to receive a wide range of support from emergency assistance and home care to management services, mental health counseling, a friendly visitor, an invitation to the holiday events.

In the last couple of years, Mrs. G's dementia unfortunately worsened and her daughter, who receives daily mental health services, had increasing medical and psychiatric problems.

In light of this emergency situation, Schechter Holocaust Services spearheaded communications with Mrs. G's only family, her deceased husband's nephew and niece. They then worked with her relatives and with State programs. Finally, after months of effort, they found a place in a lovely assisted living facility for her and a nursing home for her daughter. Mother and daughter continue to visit each other.

Schechter Holocaust Services states that it was a combination of private funding and Claims Conference funding that enabled them to help Mrs. G. I believe Mrs. G's story reflects the remarkable capacity of the individuals and the organizations that care for the survivor population.

That being said, many survivors do not seek or have access to these types of services. Further, I have heard repeated complaints that the Social Security Administration employees, at times, seem insensitive to the needs of this community and insist upon having survivors secure pensions from their former Soviet Union. This, quite frankly, is unacceptable.

For this reason, I look forward to hearing our witnesses' insights today as well as recommendations on overcoming existing impediments to accessing not only the care and assistance that they deserve, but, also, the necessary information about the family businesses and assets in Nazi-occupied areas as well.

Thank you for being here.

And, with that, I yield back, Madam Chairman.

Ms. ROS-LEHTINEN. Thank you so much, Mr. Keating.

Now I would like to recognize members for any opening statements they might like to make.

And we start with Mr. Chabot of Ohio.

Mr. CHABOT. Thank you, Madam Chairman, for holding this very important hearing.

I was in Poland and Lithuania just about 3 weeks ago. And while in Poland, we drove out to Treblinka and saw the location where about 900,000 lives, mostly Jewish, were eliminated in about a year's period of time. It was a very moving experience.

And while in Vilnius, Lithuania, we met with a survivor there who told us what had basically happened there, and she was one of the—she escaped literally the day when the Nazis were coming in to exterminate the people there.

And she escaped and spent the rest of the war with the partisans and survived. She was 93 years old and a very impressive young woman. Just incredible. Very—just a little woman. Not a young woman. A little woman.

But, in any event, I also had the opportunity to meet with government officials there. And when I raised this particular issue, having talked with some folks prior to this codel, I got an indication of how difficult a process it is in trying to facilitate the recovery of assets of Holocaust survivors.

The Poles maintain that they lost more than anybody in World War II, 3 million Poles dead, including 90 percent of the Jewish population, and that much of the property theft that took place in areas are no longer part of Poland, they claim, and they are Belarus and Germany and Eastern Ukraine, for example. Our Ambassador, who has worked extensively on the issue, told our delegation that some cases have taken 20 to 30 years to decide.

When I brought up the issue to a top Polish Government official, he expressed some frustration with the process, but said—and I am quoting here—''We are proud of what we have done. It takes time,'' not particularly encouraging.

So I hope we can discuss this afternoon how we can encourage the involved parties and governments to improve the adjudication process so it doesn't take such an unconscionably long time and that property can be more expeditiously restored to the survivors and descendants of the rightful owners.

I yield back. Thank you.

Ms. ROS-LEHTINEN. Well done—well said.

Mr. Schneider is recognized.

Mr. SCHNEIDER. Thank you, Madam Chairman. I want to thank the chairmen of both subcommittees and the ranking members for calling this very important hearing, for our witnesses today for sharing both their experiences and their insights on this critical issue.

Twenty-four years ago I had the opportunity to visit Poland and the camps of Auschwitz, others, with survivors. I was in Krakow. I recall the priests from Krakow for the first time to a Jewish group publicly apologizing for—and taking some responsibility.

The hearing today, the conversations we have had now for generations, has been about justice. And 3 weeks ago, in synagogues around the world, Jews read from the Torah portion Shoftim, one of the lines of which is ''Justice, justice shall you pursue.''

This hearing is about pursuing justice and not stopping until—and I will repeat the words of my colleague—the survivors have the care that they need, the justice that they deserve. This is what we are here today for.

I thank you for your commitment and willingness to be here to share your stories. I look forward to the rest of this hearing.

Thank you.

Ms. ROS-LEHTINEN. Thank you, sir.

Mr. Cicilline of Rhode Island.

Mr. CICILLINE. Thank you, Madam Chair. And thank you for your leadership on this incredibly important issue.

And I also thank the ranking member for his strong and persistent leadership on this issue and for his very eloquent opening remarks.

I just want to extend my gratitude to the witnesses who are here today to provide testimony to this committee.

And I particularly want to thank and welcome Mr. Rubin because I am certain that sharing his personal experience will be a painful experience. And thank you for your willingness to do that again and for being before the committee.

As we all recognize, the events of the Holocaust are one of the worst atrocities known to man where 6 million individuals were systematically murdered by the Nazis. And we have an obligation not only to remember that, but to be sure that we do all that we can to ensure that the survivors of this unspeakable moment in human history are both cared for and provided with all the dignity and justice they so richly deserve.

So I welcome the witnesses and look forward to hearing the testimony.

I yield back.

Ms. Ros-Lehtinen. Thank you, Mr. Cicilline.

Mr. Vargas.

Mr. Vargas. Thank you very much, Madam Chair.

And thank you, ranking members and chairs, for being here today.

I would associate myself with all the comments made here today. I would also say that, in San Diego, we have had this wonderful program where Holocaust survivors have gone to the schools and have talked to the children.

I have been in on a number of those talks, and I remember one that moved me very deeply when they talked about—the person that was there talked about all the things that did not happen in the world because we lost 6, 8 million Jews, all the things that didn't happen in Qualcomm in San Diego. They said there could have been 10 Qualcomms. We could have discovered so many things. So much was lost to humanity.

And so I am here to help in any way I can. And I thank very much the witnesses here, and I look forward to again hearing your testimony and helping in any way I can.

Thank you, Madam Chair.

Ms. Ros-Lehtinen. Thank you, Mr. Vargas.

Mr. Connolly.

Mr. Connolly. Thank you, Madam Chairman. And thank you for holding this hearing.

There aren't words to describe the horror of the Holocaust, and Mr. Rubin gives testimony to the fact that this is not ancient history. This happened not so long ago, as measured by history. And two words really come to my mind about the response. One is there has to still be accountability and then, secondly, there has to be expiation.

We still find treasures robbed from Jewish victims that show up in museums, that show up in auction houses, show up in private collections.

Just the other day, an individual in his 90s was fingered for having participated in atrocities during the Holocaust. So this is not something far away, and it is something that we must address and never forget.

I thank both the chairman and ranking member for their holding this hearing and for their eloquent commitment to this issue.

Ms. ROS-LEHTINEN. Thank you, Mr. Connolly.

And now we are pleased to introduce our witnesses.

First are—both of our subcommittees are pleased to welcome Mr. Jack Rubin, who survived the atrocities of the Holocaust.

In 1944, Mr. Rubin was deported to the Beregsastz Ghetto. From there, he was once again deported to Auschwitz, where he was liberated in May 1945. Jack was fortunate enough to come to America, and he served honorably and proudly in the United States Army.

Over the course of his life, Jack has reached out to other survivors and has dedicated so much of his time to creating awareness about the horrors of the Holocaust. He has testified before in many different venues, and he is joined by his son, who was kind enough to help him come here today.

Jack, we are honored with your presence.

We are also pleased to have with us Klara Firestone, who has worked with Holocaust survivors since 1978. She is a founding member of the Coordinating Committee of Generations of the Shoah International and a board member of the Los Angeles Museum of the Holocaust.

We welcome you. Thank you so much.

We are also joined by Dr. Barbara Paris, who is currently vice chair of medicine and director of the geriatrics division at the Maimonides Medical Center in New York. Dr. Paris has dedicated her life to studying the needs of survivors from clinical perspectives. Her practice is located in the neighborhood with the highest concentration of Holocaust survivors in the United States.

Welcome, Doctor.

And last, but certainly not least, we are pleased to welcome Eugenie Lieberman. Eugenie is the daughter of Iver Segalowitz, who was the only survivor of his family, the only survivor of his family. Her father invested countless hours advocating for other Holocaust survivors. Iver kept fighting his entire life until he could no longer with be us.

Our deepest condolences, Eugenie. And his fight now carries out through you.

So we welcome our distinguished panel for being with us today. We will first hear from Mr. Jack Rubin.

Your prepared statement has been made a part of the record. Please feel free to summarize as you wish.

Welcome, Jack. If you could push the button on the microphone and hold it close to your mouth so we can all hear you.

STATEMENT OF MR. JACK RUBIN (HOLOCAUST SURVIVOR)

Mr. RUBIN. Good afternoon, Madam Chairwoman Ileana Ros-Lehtinen, Ranking Member Ted Deutch.

As you know well, my name is Jack Rubin. I was born in Vari, Czechoslovakia, and I am a survivor of several Nazi concentration and death camps.

You know from our struggle dating back to the late 1990s, we survivors have tried everything we know to lift our brothers and sisters out of this grinding poverty, and little has worked.

Instead, we have been blocked everywhere we turned, in court cases right up to the Supreme Court, in Congress, and even seeking proper level funding directly from Germany.

Small and inconsistent gains over the years from Germany, channeled through The Claim Conference, are delivered uneven and inadequate ways, and we still see the poverty and misery at tragically high levels still today.

After all, out of 110,000 survivors alive in the United States, some 55,000 are living near or below accepted levels of poverty. The present system and funding available simply perpetuated the status quo and will not uplift survivors from their present tragic situation.

We have struggled, along with our members in Congress, in our fight all the way to stop this tragedy of survivors living in poverty for over 15 years, and we have not succeeded. In 1 minute to midnight now, my friends, a solution must be found to stop this tragedy now, once and for all.

As we have said here in the Senate over and over, the time has come to secure realistic funding level for the clinical mandated services needed by survivors to lift them out from their present cruel situation and to provide them with actually services needed once and for all.

We have begged all the authorities involved in this tragedy to do the math and actually look what's being negotiated by The Claim Conference from Germany and compare the dollar results with what the doctors and the professionals have mandated for each and every survivors in dire need to alleviate their physical and mental health problems.

Right now there is a total disconnect and everybody knows it, but nothing is done to correct this horrible imbalance. And the survivors remain trapped in horrors, if not enough care, and continue their suffering.

Many well-meaning people seem to believe that piecemeal private fundraising and volunteer services is the right way to go. We know this is simply not true. Survivors should not be forced to endure more, and the same system has brought about this calamity.

Half measures cannot provide home care, for mental health care, nor medical services to treat the damages caused by the malnutrition, massive infections, and brain infections. We have real cases which would shock you.

We hope that soon enough, dear friends, there will be a lot of time to study and speak and have concerts and all those other good things, but they should not come before taking care of the human sufferings.

Please use your powerful voices to amplify our failing pleas to help those among us most in need now, and that can only happen with the government assuming full care and cost for the actual needs for our brothers and sisters continue to suffer.

Ad hoc private fundraising, U.S. taxpayers' fund, no volunteers, no matter how we are met, we will never do the actual appropriations. From Germany will do, as Chancellor Adenauer pledged. And we will never solve those tragedy survivors who are suffering.

We believe the actually unmet need for survivors care for the needs among emergency services and proper professional-based home care fund is in the billions of dollars. The only fair and decent option today is a partnership with the German Government will suffice today with guaranteed funding for the actual needs presented.

Holocaust survivors are not asking more help from the U.S. taxpayers. Survivors already benefit from many programs for the elderly and should continue to do so. We hope this can be made better for our elderly in U.S.

However, taxpayers are already burdened enough. And soon 10 million American baby boomers will be turning 65 every year for the foreseeable future.

Holocaust survivors endured ghettos, starvation, disease, concentration camps, killing factories, and death marches, came to the United States and became proud and productive American citizens. Many survivors served this country in combat in Korea and Vietnam. I myself am a U.S. military veteran.

But survivors are fiercely independent and never wanted to rely on their fellow Americans for a penny of assistance. The same survivors now have to ask for help because they can no longer care for themself.

The United States did not cause this problem for the survivors today. Nazi Germany did. Insurance companies, such as Allianz and Generale, should also be called upon to contribute to social funds because their Holocaust profits.

We are losing more and more survivors every day. The remaining survivors need our help now. We need this committee to figure out how much they need for housing, dental care, home health care, and other services, and then use your stature of power to help us secure the needed funding today without any more delays.

We need the President, the Vice President, the entire administration, this committee, and the entire Congress to pressure Germany and all culpable business entities to fulfill their moral obligations to the Holocaust survivors.

We believe this committee and our elected Members of Congress, Madam Chairman Ros-Lehtinen, and Ranking Member Deutch, in bringing your caring colleagues in the House and the Senate along with you, as Senator Nelson and Senator Boxer have done in the Senate.

Thank you, Madam Chairman and Mr. Ranking Member. We know each other too well for such formalities. You know better than anyone else what we need. Please, use this hearing as an opportunity to make a real difference for the remaining survivors who desperately need your help.

Finally, I have several important articles, letters, that I wish to be included as part of my statement for the hearing record and ask they be included.

Thank you very much.

[The prepared statement of Mr. Rubin follows:]

Statement of Jack Rubin
United States House of Representatives
Committee on Foreign Affairs Joint Subcommittee Hearing
Subcommittee on Europe, Eurasia, and Emerging Threats
Subcommittee on the Middle East and North Africa

The Struggles of Recovering Assets for Holocaust Survivors

September 18, 2014

My name is Jack Rubin. I am a survivor of several Nazi concentration and death camps, the only member of my beloved family to survive the Holocaust. Somehow I survived and was fortunate to make it to this great country and raise a beautiful family, with three (3) children and four (4) grandchildren.

I have served on the advisory committee of the Jewish Family Services in West Palm Beach for many years, and am also a member of the executive committee of the Holocaust Survivors Foundation USA, which we formed 14 years ago to fight for the rights of tens of thousands of survivors still living in the United States, especially those living in poverty. Our leaders are elected by survivors from all over the United States. I am speaking here in my individual capacity.

I begin by thanking the leadership of this Committee for giving us Holocaust survivors and the family members of Holocaust survivors the opportunity to speak here about what we have experienced and continue to experience. We thank Chairman Royce and Ranking Member Engel, Chairman Rohrabacher and Ranking Member Keating, and Chairwoman Ros-Lehtinen and Ranking Member Deutch. We are very proud of our South Florida representatives working with the other important leaders of this Congress, and would like to specially acknowledge the many, many years of dynamic and critical support that Ileana Ros-Lehtinen and Ted Deutch have given to the Holocaust survivors in the United States, Europe, Israel, and everywhere else survivors live.

As you know from our struggles dating back to the late 1990s, we survivors have tried everything we know to lift our brothers and sisters out of this grinding poverty and little has worked.

Instead, we have been blocked everywhere we have turned, in court cases right up the Supreme Court, in Congress, and even seeking proper funding directly from Germany. The small and inconsistent gains in funding for survivors over the years from Germany, channeled through the Claims Conference, are delivered in uneven and we believe inadequate ways, and we still see the poverty and misery at tragically high levels still today.

Some 55,000 Holocaust survivors in the United States today live near or below the official federal poverty level. This is tragic and unacceptable. We believe that a serious assessment by this Committee of the actual cost of needed in-home care and basic emergency services such as medicines, dental care, hearing aids, food, rent, utilities, transportation, and other vital services will show a multi-billion dollar deficit.

The Holocaust survivors in this country strongly believe even at this very late date, we must return to the origins of Chancellor Adenauer's promise in the 1950's when he said that modern Germany must take care of the all of the needs of survivors due to the savage actions of the predecessor government, the Nazi German regime, with the death camps, the labor camps, medical experiments, torture, and other crimes which have left this tragic legacy till this very hour. Because of the these horrible deprivations, survivors' mental and physical health care needs are more extensive, more complex, and more dire than other elderly people, and require serious, comprehensive responses.

Unfortunately, the existing system has fallen tragically short of what survivors need and deserve. The current funding and care delivery system is difficult for survivors to access, and also severely underfunded.

Holocaust survivors are looking to this Committee to help secure the funding for the care all survivors need, primarily from the German government and businesses such as Allianz and Generali who profited from the Holocaust. Survivors are not seeking additional funds from the United States government or American taxpayers, or from Jewish philanthropy. The United States did not cause survivors' extensive problems we experience today, and neither did the Jewish community. Looking to these sources is wrong in principle and wrong because it will never yield the amount of funds actually needed to provide for the needs of survivors today.

Here are some examples collected from South Florida and other communities throughout the U.S.:

- Emergency funds are capped at $2,500 per year per survivor. That is a cap, not a guarantee. Most survivors get less every year because of limited funds that have to be divided among many survivors with emergencies. The result is that many, many survivors' emergency needs go unmet.

- Hearing aids usually cost about $5,000, and are not covered by Medicare. With the $2,500 cap and lower actual amounts available, survivors often cannot get even one hearing aid, much less two in the same year. How can a hearing impaired survivor in his or her late 80s be expected to manage with no or only one hearing aid?

- Most survivors have extensive dental needs because during the Holocaust, we had no opportunity to care for our teeth, suffered extreme malnutrition, as well as beatings and other horrible deprivations. Unfortunately, dental services are paid for from the same emergency funds that are limited to $2,500 per year. And the dental work that many survivors need costs thousands and thousands of dollars. Some dentists give pro bono help in some cities, but this is very limited. I see and hear story after story where survivors cannot get the gum surgery, or extensive dental work they need because there is no money. This is a very, very big problem. The lack of proper dental care harms survivors' dignity, and also puts them at risk for bad nutrition and cardiac problems.

- Many poor survivors don't have a car, cannot access public transportation, or cannot drive themselves to medical appointments. The lack of transportation to go to the doctor is a real problem and there is not enough money for this. Survivors often miss their doctor appointments for lack of transportation.

- The cap on home care funds has been reduced in some areas by 50%. In some cases survivors with documented need of 24 hour care had funding cut from $2,500 to $1,250 per month.

- There is the elderly survivor, Mrs. K, who is very sick and is in the hospital for blood transfusions, but was refused when she asked for her AARP insurance paid which she couldn't afford – all of $625 for a quarter

- Or, Mrs. I, who needed a refrigerator and after a six week wait, her application was denied. This was in September and she still does not have a working refrigerator for her food and medicine.

- There was the elderly survivor woman who, during one of the hottest days of this past summer, requested money for an air conditioner that cost $500. She was told they only had enough money to give her half of the cost. Unfortunately she didn't have the rest and had to endure the unbearable summer heat without air conditioning.

- There is the survivor who was desperate for assistance to pay for a stair lift since her husband is home bound and was told they were too rich for assistance, even though their mortgage payments use up most of their income.

- Survivors are begging for home care and being refused. In one community I was told the maximum is 15 hours per week, despite the severity of the survivors' illness. These are people who are not eligible for Medicaid. If they go to an assisted living facility, they use every penny available to pay their overhead, but you have to know that aids in those facilities cost extra. The Claims Conference programs refuse any assistance to survivors for these so-called "extra" services in assisted living facilities or nursing homes.

- These many problems are illustrated by the case of a survivor from Stovnietze, Poland, who spent World War II in the Lodz and Kielce ghettos, and Auschwitz. He survived because he was a mechanic and also learned to be a bricklayer. He suffered so many injuries in the camps including terrible foot injuries from standing barefoot in the snow. Everyone but his sister perished in the camps. This survivor eventually settled in Richmond, Virginia. He worked all his life and had saved some money, but never married and had no children. But like many survivors, he was a hoarder. As he aged it got so bad he was pinned down in his home. When neighbors didn't see his car move for three days, they called the police, who had to hoist this elderly survivor out the upstairs window. He was sent to the hospital close to death. Showing signs of recovery, he got better in a nursing home until his medical coverage came to an end. He couldn't move home because it was unlivable, so he went to assisted living, at $5,000 a month, which increased to $6,000 as he faltered. Soon he needed aides in the facility, which cost an additional $6,000 per month -- with no assistance from the Claims Conference or other programs. These costs were far beyond his reach financially. He had to be moved to another facility that was less expensive, where he eventually died in March 2013. However, without the help of a group of two very dedicated friends and his former employer in the small Richmond community he would never have received the attention or care he needed.

- Widows and widowers who live alone cannot get home care from Medicare if they don't spend a certain number of nights in the hospital, and after many operations are told they should have help at home even if there were only in the hospital overnight. Yet the rationing of home care funds puts these survivors in danger.

- Some survivors are now applying for assistance for the first time. This is because they are desperate for help, but their needs were not factored into the agency's budget and they have to wait for help which may never come. Others do not even apply because they are aware of the funding shortages.

- Survivors are re-traumatized every time they have to retell their wartime experiences and for many, the application process for assistance is emotionally brutal.

- Though there are fewer survivors every year, the agencies caseloads are increasing because more are becoming poor, they are getting more frail, and their needs are increasing due to declining health.

- It is unconscionable that survivors, who went hungry for years during the Holocaust, should go hungry in the United States, but they are.

- If a survivor moves to an assisted living facility or a nursing facility, the Claims Conference programs provide no assistance if they need help with a personal aide or with personal hygiene. If a survivor lives independently, he or she can get meals delivered or other services, but these stop if they move to a facility. In these facilities, a resident must pay extra for assistance with meds or to take a bath, but none of that is covered by the Claims Conference.

- Social workers and survivors involved in the advisory committees have heard this question far too often: "Do I take my medication or do I buy food?" There are limited funds that must cover a broad range of needs. "Should the agency take care of every need of a few survivors, or take care of some needs of many survivors?" Under the current framework, these questions are inevitable. Rationing is inevitable. Why does it have to be this way?

- There are children of survivors who are putting themselves in financial jeopardy to help care for their parents. We are grateful that the Committee recognized this problem and invited Ms. Bar-Cohen to relate her personal experience in caring for her father. These difficulties are widespread.

Doing the Math to Properly Analyze Recent German Home Care Announcement

Madame Chairwoman, and Mr. Ranking Member, you are well aware from our many years of work that in-home care is vital for survivors as they cannot be institutionalized easily whether it be a nursing home or mental health facility, which conjures up for most survivors the most bitter memories of the way the Nazis treated us. There could be nothing worse than having to be institutionalized after all we experienced.

You have heard our pleas for over a decade, seeking a dedicated, permanent source of funding for long-germ care whose access survivors could control themselves. As you are well aware, these plans have been repeatedly blocked by the institutions that preferred the status quo. Think of the thousands who have suffered since then who could have been helped if the past efforts you supported had not been derailed! I raise this not to assess blame, but to remind you and the Committee that survivors need and deserve comprehensive, accurate, and **survivor-centered solutions – TODAY.**

Now everyone is talking about home care, with grand announcements that Germany would spend $800 million over the next four years (2014-2017) for survivors' home care through the Claims Conference. We are asking the Committee to please take a very close look at this announcement and use a sharp pencil and paper to really understand what it will mean to survivors for tangible help they desperately need.

According to the announcements 56,000 survivors per year are served via the Claims Conference with these German funds. This 56,000 number does not include untold numbers of other survivors who are not currently served, because we know most agencies do not conduct or cannot afford outreach because funds for services are already limited. Yet these Holocaust survivors are also entitled to help and they must be an integral part of this calculation, too.

But if the Committee and the Congress do the simple math, it will show how terribly inadequate these supposedly large dollar figures are when it comes to the reality of what the survivors really need.

$200 million per year divided by the 56,000 survivors that the Claims Conference and Germany say are now being served, amounts to about $3,560 for each Holocaust survivor each year.

The average survivor in his or her 80s needs at least 15 hours per week of home care. At $15 per hour, which would be the low end in Chicago and South Florida, $3,560 only provides 16 weeks a year of home care. What is a survivor supposed to do the other 36 weeks?

If a survivor needs 24 hour a day care, the new German fund would provide only 9 days of care every year.

In New York City, where home care costs at least $20 per hour, the funds would provide even less home care for Holocaust survivors.

This is obviously not sufficient. Survivors cannot make it on partial solutions, press releases, and political rhetoric.

A recent report of the New York City social services organization Self Help shows how inadequate the recently announced funding levels really are. It says that in 2013, in the New York City metropolitan area alone, 26,572 survivors, or 41% of the New York survivor population, required some help with daily tasks. When that number is compared with the 56,000 survivors worldwide that are currently "served" via home care funds through the Claims Conference, the deficiencies are obvious. New York accounts for roughly half of the U.S. survivor population, which is between 20 and 25% of the world survivor population. If New York's survivor population, with about 12% of the world's total, has enough survivors needing home care to comprise (for analytical purposes) 47% of the total number of survivors getting help with home care through the Claims Conference today, the "math" shows there are huge amounts of unmet needs now, and will be gaping needs in the years to come.

When viewed in historical context, the recent German home care announcement is even more chilling. This grand new announcement might meet 25% of survivors' current home care needs. However, it is the culmination of several years of increases since 2005 in which the totals have doubled with each new announcement, usually every two years. Since the latest, high-water mark will only meet 25% of U.S. survivors' home care needs, it shows how much unnecessary suffering survivors had to endure in recent years as funding has been inching up gradually through negotiations with Germany without regard for the **actual** human needs being neglected.

Another question this Committee should ask is: What are the Claims Conference's plans for the new German home care funds? Have the allocations for each city in the United States been determined? We think that the United States House of Representatives and the Senate, and certainly the Holocaust survivors and our families, are entitled to know exactly how the new German home care funds will be allocated -- where, when, and how much? The same is true for all other funds for all the other needs survivors continue to need so badly.

Doing this math, taking the local pay scales of any local venue, X$/hour for home health care workers X number of days a month which are clinically determined to be needed, gives you a number which makes a mockery of the actions and proposals currently on the table. The unique health and emotional conditions and illnesses of survivors require professional treatments. We think a serious, intensive, and critical inquiry will show the actual need is several billion dollars for home care alone, when you consider the aggregate, world wide need, and the remaining years this care will be needed, and a like amount for emergency services also. Where will the funding come from for these desperately needed professional services when Germany's recent, highly publicized increases still yield only 25% of the funds needed into the foreseeable future?

Survivors need mental health care in much larger proportion than do any other population directly because of what was done to them – to us -- under the Nazi German regime for years. Many competent health care professionals prescribe measures to help and there is little money to help leaving survivors alone to contend with the sleeplessness, nightmares and horrors being relived over and over. Only recently, the Claims Conference announced the results of recent negotiations with the German Government resulting in a one time payment for Child Survivors for the first time amounting to $3,280 total. Once again, the negotiations and public relations surrounding the announcement leave the impression of a very important result but in fact the math shows a huge false impression. What are survivors and their families to do to get help once again with such negotiations results with Germany not paying the actual funding to care for their horrid needs directly resulting from what the Nazi Germans did to them?

I very much doubt that Chancellor Adenauer, who promised in the 1950s that Germany would provide for the victims of the Holocaust "to their last breath," would be satisfied by the state of affairs today.

Survivors need and deserve a realistic German rational funding that will address all important unmet needs, ideally worldwide. It should no longer be acceptable to cause continuing misery to survivors based on piecemeal negotiations every few years and a patchwork of programs.

I would add here that the problems of survivors living in poverty and suffering without the care they need is a worldwide problem – including in Israel where over 40% of the world's Holocaust survivors live. The issue is of such concern in Israel that, even as the people of Israel braced for war with Hamas this past July, the *Jerusalem Post* published a statement I wrote addressing the depth of the problems facing Holocaust survivors in the U.S., Israel, and worldwide. In that article, I wrote:

> Survivors and second and third generation leaders have long opposed the current cynical framework pitting the heirs of East German properties against indigent survivors. This shell game, enabled by the silence bought by Claims Conference grants, has allowed the Claims Conference to protect Germany while maintaining monopoly control over Holocaust-related assets and survivors' welfare. But the fact is, Germany caused the massive medical and emotional problems survivors are confronting today, and Germany should pay for all of the survivors' needs, without the bargaining and compromising that has become the Claims Conference's specialty. Survivors and heirs should have the right to recover their lost assets, including German properties, insurance claims, and artworks, and Germany should pay for the needs of indigent survivors.

http://www.jpost.com/Opinion/Op-Ed-Contributors/Memo-to-the-Claims-Conference-We-Holocaust-survivors-are-not-dead-yet-362041

In connection with this statement and my live testimony, I request that the Committee accept some letters and other materials concerning this and the other matters I have addressed here.

Survivors Are Not Asking for Help from U.S. Taxpayers

Members of this Committee and Subcommittees, we want to also be clear that Holocaust survivors are not asking for more help from the U.S. taxpayers. Survivors already benefit from many programs for the elderly, and should continue to do so. We hope these can be made better for all elderly in the U.S. However, U.S. taxpayers are already burdened enough, and soon 10 million American baby boomers will be turning 65 every year for the foreseeable future. Shaving off thin slices of these precious funds which themselves have been sequestered and cut along with regularly targeted funds added would make it tragic for survivors to be inserted in that long line of those seeking those ever smaller funds.

Holocaust survivors endured ghettos, starvation, disease, concentration camps, killing factories, and death marches. We came to the United States and became proud and productive American citizens. Many survivors served this country in combat in Korea and Vietnam. I myself am a U.S. military veteran. Survivors are fiercely independent and never wanted to rely on their fellow Americans for a penny of assistance. These same survivors now have to ask for help because they can no longer care for themselves.

But the United States did not cause the problems survivors face today – Germany did.

As a survivor I am sick as are my colleagues that these taxpayer funds of HHS, and others are being contemplated for use for us and our brothers and sisters when we insist Germany's full responsibility to provide the actual costs of all the services remains a moral and a practical imperative.

In this regard, I feel it is necessary to comment on the recent initiative announced by the White House about helping Holocaust survivors.

The White House announced an "initiative" to help Holocaust survivors in need with a plan to appoint one desk person at HHS to coordinate with social service agencies, begin a program to recruit VISTA volunteers to help survivors, and begin to organize fundraising in the Jewish Federations to augment funding for survivors' needs.

As it currently stands, the White House's announcement is deeply flawed. Survivors deserve the most thorough, professional, and comprehensive care available, not half-measures. And the Jewish community should not be looked to for fundraising to fill these gaps – the Jewish people were the victims, not the perpetrators. The Jewish communities should not be called upon today to provide the financial assistance that is Germany's responsibility, and be asked to short-change other community priorities such as Jewish education, youth programs of all kinds, providing assistance for other Jews in need locally and throughout the world, including other Jewish elderly, and most recently, Israel's humanitarian needs during and after the war with Hamas.

It isn't like the Jewish Federations have not been aware of the shortages in funding for survivors over the past several years. They too have been hit hard by the economy, and changing philanthropic trends and lack of confidence in institutions as well. Further, many communities have tried to hold special fundraising efforts, which are well-intended but never calculated to nor have they succeeded in actually raising the funds to provide survivors the full measure of assistance needed.

The survivors' needs are vast and immediate. Why should we Holocaust survivors always be subjected to these kinds of compromises and flawed solutions? Well-meaning but short-sighted suggestions that survivors' needs can be addressed through volunteer programs and extra fundraising in Jewish communities will not suffice.

We raised all of these concerns with the Vice President's staff, and these are only some of the reasons we believe the White House's announcement should be viewed as perhaps a starting point, but not the end point for what is needed to provide the complete and professional levels of care that survivors need and deserve, and not to sidetrack a the urgent business to immediately get this right for survivors, at long last. This is in every sense of the word, a matter of life and death. Where is the urgency?

If there is more Federal Government support or more charitable contributions to help some of the survivors in need as we all know about, it would be welcome. But this is not the solution to the vast problems survivors face today. This approach has been tried for decades and it has not worked. When we are talking about needing hundreds of millions of dollars per year over and above what is currently being spent to properly care for survivors, raising a few million dollars in the Jewish community will not come close to solving the problem, and neither will $5 million or $10 million from the U.S. government.

If only all these well-meaning friends would simply do the math to understand how survivors real, medically mandated health care could never be met under those solutions thus far put in place. The Government of Germany is the only source of realistic levels of funding to make a difference in the lives of survivors living in poverty. The good-sounding negotiations results simply will never do that.

This past May, the Administration's Special Envoy for Holocaust Issues, and her colleagues, travelled to South Florida to meet with the survivor community, the adult children of survivors many of whom are caretakers, and the Jewish Family and Children's' Services professionals who have the prime responsibility to administer what little funds exist for survivors. These meetings took place in Miami, Fort Lauderdale, Boca Raton, and West Palm Beach. I am proud that in each community the survivors and family members were united in our report: there is simply not enough funding available to meet the needs that we know about much less the problems faced by so many destitute survivors too embarrassed to seek help.

While we were encouraged by the caring attitude that the Administration's people brought, we are very concerned that their agenda is far too limited, i.e. focused solely on making federal programs work better for survivors. Well, that is a laudable and long overdue goal, and we offered what support we could. However, it would be tragic of the Administration lost sight of the big picture and the urgency of the needs of survivors today which can only be addressed by substantial increases in funding from Germany and other culpable Holocaust countries and profiteers. We implored the White House representatives to urge the President and Vice President to take a leadership position and bring our concerns to Chancellor Merkel personally.

We know social service agencies and local leaders throughout the United States charged with the responsibility to provide care for survivors have to manage with insufficient resources. But their hands seem to be tied when it comes to the most significant obstacles facing survivors. Why don't they speak up and support the survivors seeking to hold Germany responsible for providing the complete current amounts of funds survivors desperately need. Why do retired German WWII veterans and even SS officers receive ample pensions and complete health care coverage, when Holocaust survivors are forced to choose between paying for food or medicine, and cannot pay for dental care, home care, utilities, home care, and other basic needs? This isn't right.

Maybe, after this hearing and the Committee's work, the White House will immediately build on the acknowledgement that the needs are great, and use its unique authority to deliver the comprehensive financial support that survivors need and deserve.

However, even without the White House, we believe in this Committee and in our elected members of Congress, led by you Congresswoman Ros-Lehtinen and Congressman Deutch, and the 100-plus other members of this House who have previously supported the Holocaust survivors. We ask that you initiate an effort with them to raise your collective voices with Germany, as Senators Nelson and Boxer have done in the Senate.

Please, Madame Chairwoman and Mr. Ranking Member and Members of this Committee, help us by contacting Chancellor Merkel and your counterparts in the German Parliament, the Bundestag, to get this message understood once and for all. Otherwise, we will die never seeing meaningful help provided to the tens of thousands of brothers and sisters who need help but continue to suffer.

We are losing more and more survivors every day and they need our help now. We need to this Committee to figure out how much they need for housing, dental care, home health care and other survivors and then use your eminence as members of this great United States Senate to help us secure the needed funding, today, without any more delays. The German government and the United States government continues to protect the Allianz insurance company and to hide behind the Claims Conference in providing insufficient levels of care for tens of thousands of survivors in need. We need the Vice President, the entire Administration, this Committee and entire Congress to pressure Germany, and all culpable business entities, to fulfill their moral obligations to Holocaust survivors, today.

What Happened After the 1997 Senate Resolution Calling on Germany to Provide Adequate Income Support and Full Health Care for Holocaust Survivors?

In 1997, the United States Senate unanimously passed a resolution co-sponsored by Senators Moynihan, Graham, Hatch, Dodd, and Biden, calling on Germany to provide adequate material and social service support so that *all Holocaust survivors* could live in dignity. The resolution noted that retired SS officers in Germany and elsewhere receive far more generous health care benefits from Germany than Holocaust survivors. It called for, among other goals, that "the German Government should fulfill its responsibilities to victims of the Holocaust and immediately set up a comprehensive medical fund to cover the medical expenses of all Holocaust survivors worldwide." S.Con. Res. 39, July 15, 1997.

Unfortunately, neither the Jewish community leadership, the Executive Branch, nor Congress followed through on persuading Germany to live up to these aspirations. Today, 17 years later, there is no more excuse for delay.

The grandstanding, fractured, and irrational, bi-annual announcements of Claims Conference-German secret negotiations have got to stop as the means of caring for survivors once and for all. It should be replaced by the serious solution sought by the survivors who have pleaded for this for nearly 15 years of agony and endless suffering and inability to lift their brothers and sisters in need into a reasonably comfortable and dignified quality of life, and having watched as so many survivors died in agony these past 15 years while those in power ignored or failed to grasp the seriousness of our plight. The above suggested process is the only way once and for all to set the process right and kill poverty among our ranks before it is too late.

Data on Survivors Living in Poverty

When the group of survivor leaders who eventually started the Holocaust Survivors Foundation USA started this effort back in 1998, 1999, 2000, there were at least 87,500 U.S. survivors living in or near poverty, which was half of the 175,000 living survivors in the U.S. at the time. Today, there are some 110,000 living survivors, and still, half – 55,000 – live below the poverty line or are considered poor. To us survivors, it is unbearable to think about the tens of thousands of survivors who already died in misery in this great country without the care they needed. It is unconscionable that thousands of survivors, who went hungry for years during the Holocaust, should have died hungry or alone here in these great United States. The current framework is not acceptable, and never was. But now that this Committee is investigating the status of survivors in the United States, we are praying that this Committee's work will not allow the catastrophes of the past decade to be repeated.

Keep in mind that Holocaust survivors also suffer from much higher levels of poverty than other elderly because of the loss of parents, grandparents, the loss of property and other assets, and the deprivation of educational opportunities. Even many survivors who did OK economically have outlived their resources, and are now unable to afford the care they need.

Unfortunately, there is no comprehensive census data that shows the number of survivors in the U.S., the number that live in poverty, and the kind of care they are receiving via government and privately-delivered services. However, there are several local studies and national surveys that support the basic finding that half of all survivors live below or near the poverty level, and that the funding for survivors' needs is terribly inadequate everywhere. Here are a few of these summarized.

National Data. As I noted, today, some 55,000 Holocaust survivors in the U.S. – half of the survivor population here – live below or near the poverty line and cannot afford sufficient food, shelter, medicine, health care, home care, dental care, hearing aids, eyeglasses, and other services necessary for a dignified old age. This number is derived from data from leading demographers compiled by the Jewish Federation system and filed with the Federal Court in 2004. The number of U.S. survivors living in or near poverty at the time was 87,500. (*See* Sheskin, Estimates of the Number of Nazi Victims and Their Economic Status, January 2004; 2000-01 National Jewish Population Survey.) 55,000 is also the number cited by the Claims Conference when describing the population of U.S. survivors who are poor today.

Los Angeles. In December 2008, the Jewish Federation of Los Angeles conducted a survey which concluded that there are 10,000-12,000 Holocaust survivors living in the Los Angeles metropolitan area, most of whom are over the age of 85, 75% of whom are female, and 49% of whom are "low income or poor." *See* Los Angeles Community Study of Vulnerable Jewish Seniors and Holocaust Survivors, December 2008.

The Los Angeles study found, "[c]onsistent with other national studies, Holocaust survivors in Los Angeles are less affluent than other Jews, with 49% of households either low-income or poor. Using the federal poverty guidelines, 27% of survivors are living at or below 100% of the guidelines."

New York. A few years ago, the UJA-Federation of New York City reported that "[t]here are 73,000 aging Holocaust survivors in NY, half of whom are living at or below the poverty level." *See* http://www.facebook.com/ujafedny.

As I said before, a recent report in 2013 by Self Help found that in 2013, in the New York City metropolitan area alone, **26,572** survivors, or 41% of the New York survivor population, required some help with daily tasks.

San Francisco. The *Jewish News Weekly of Northern California* reported in 2008 that of 4,000 Holocaust survivors living in the Bay Area, 1,000 of them "are in trouble," and that "the Jewish community is not raising enough money to care for the poorest and sickest in a proper and humane way." *See* Anita Friedman, "Holocaust Remembrance is About Honoring the Living, Too," *Jewish News Weekly of Northern California*, May 2, 2008. These concerns about the large number of survivors in need in the Bay Area were again reported four years later. *See* Deborah Garel, "As We Memorialize Shoah Victims, Don't Forget the Living," *Jweekly.com*, April 12, 2012.

Washington, D.C. The *Washington (D.C.) Jewish Week* reported in November 2012 that while "Claims Conference money has never been enough to fund the JSSA's (Jewish Social Services Agency's) support for Holocaust survivors," that in 2012 the agency was estimating a $500,000 shortfall because of the increased demand for services. *See* "Fiscal Cliff for Survivors," *The Washington Jewish Week*, November 28, 2012.

South Florida. In Miami, a 2003 survey (the most recent one to ask the question) found that 39% of survivors live below the official poverty level. No one believes the situation has improved since then. But the community isn't even asking the question now – either to avoid embarrassment, or perhaps because they realize the results won't make a difference with today's funding system.

In preparation for the 2009 Prague Conference on Holocaust Assets, the South Florida social service organizations met with the Holocaust survivor leadership and Congresswoman Ileana Ros-Lehtinen to discuss the conditions facing survivors in the care of the communities there. In Miami, the director reported that the survivors under the care of the Jewish Community Services organization are mostly in their late 80s and 90s, and require substantially greater care on the whole than they did even a few years ago, but the current system only provides a portion of the hours of home care needed.

Broward County and Palm Beach Counties reported larger but somewhat younger survivor populations, with slightly lower levels of poverty levels and lower levels of hours of care and emergency services needed on average. So, Broward and Palm Beach Counties' survivors were at the time of that meeting getting about one quarter to one third of the home care they needed, about 4-6 hours per week (like Miami 10 years ago). Further, their emergency funds from the Claims Conference are not only rationed every month, but run out long before the end of the year. Because their situations mirror what Miami looked like a decade ago, we can assume the needs will continue to grow among survivors there in the coming years.

I am including a current write-up from the Alpert Jewish Family & Children's Service organization in West Palm Beach as an exhibit to my testimony.

Israel and elsewhere. There are also thousands of impoverished Holocaust survivors living in Israel, Europe, Canada, Australia, and South America who are not receiving the services they need for a dignified quality of life. According to the Claims Conference in 2010, the number of Holocaust survivors living in or near poverty in Israel was 74,000, and the number in the former Soviet Union was 90,000. When the 55,000 poor U.S. survivors are included in this ghastly count, it shows **219,000 Holocaust survivors living in or near poverty worldwide**. As has been widely reported to the shock and dismay of many, even survivors in Israel do not receive proper and needed care, due to funding shortages from Claims Conference and the Israeli government, it doesn't. *See, e.g.* Liel Leibovitz, "Israel's Starving Survivors," *Tablet*, April 8, 2013; Daniel Ziri, "Budget Runs Out for Holocaust Survivors' Expenses," *The Jerusalem Post*, August 11, 2012.

Insurance Companies' Responsibility

Congresswoman Ros-Lehtinen and Congressman Deutch, we also appreciate your introducing HR 890 in 2011 and pushing as hard as you did to have it pass through this Committee and go further. That bill would have restored Holocaust survivors' rights to sue Allianz, Generali, AXA, Munich Re, Swiss Re, Zurich, Basler, RAS, Victoria, and other global insurers who dishonored insurance policies they sold to our parents and grandparents. The failure of your bill to advance to even a floor vote in the House (and of S. 466 to advance to a vote in the Senate Judiciary Committee) remains a bitter disappointment to Holocaust survivors and our families. I would like my testimony before the 2008 Senate Foreign Affairs Committee, and the testimony of fellow HSF executive committee member Renee Firestone in the House and Senate in 2011 and 2012, along with my other HSF colleagues who have testified on the insurance issue and other issues of vital concern to survivors, to be deemed an official part of this hearing record. Here are the citations:

http://www.foreign.senate.gov/imo/media/doc/RubinJTestimony080506p1.pdf

http://archives.republicans.foreignaffairs.house.gov/112/fir111611.pdf

http://www.judiciary.senate.gov/pdf/12-6-20FirestoneTestimony.pdf

http://democrats.foreignaffairs.house.gov/110/rec032807.htm

http://archives.republicans.foreignaffairs.house.gov/112/71263.pdf

http://judiciary.house.gov/hearings/pdf/Dubbin100922.pdf

http://archives.financialservices.house.gov/hearing110/arbeiter020708.pdf

http://archives.republicans.foreignaffairs.house.gov/110/sch032807.htm

http://archives.republicans.foreignaffairs.house.gov/110/rec032807.htm

http://www.gpo.gov/fdsys/pkg/CHRG-110hhrg38141/pdf/CHRG-110hhrg38141.pdf

http://archives.republicans.foreignaffairs.house.gov/110/mos100307.htm

http://archives.republicans.foreignaffairs.house.gov/110/rub100307.htm

The reason is that my colleagues and I have attempted to bring the concerns of the survivor community before this Congress over the past decade on several occasions, and our positions have been thoroughly documented and supported. But we have been overwhelmed by the moneyed interests of the insurance companies, the misrepresentations of the Bush and Obama Administrations, and the treachery and dishonesty of certain non-survivor Jewish groups led by the Claims Conference, ADL, AJC, B'nai B'rith, Agudas Israel, the World Jewish Congress, and Stuart Eizenstat.

But insurers collectively owe Holocaust survivors and our families well over $20 billion in today's dollars, and they have denied us our families' historic and financial legacies. Thousands of survivors have died as second class citizens in this country without the ability to reclaim their families' financial and historic legacies. It is criminal that the insurers remain immune, with the assistance of those I just named.

I raise this here for several reasons. First, even if survivors' legal rights were restored and all traceable beneficiaries and heirs are paid, there would still be billions of dollars in likely heirless proceeds these companies could and should contribute to a fund to assist survivors today. As I said in 2008, what about the policies that went up in flames in Auschwitz-Birkenau, and the other death camps? Why should Generali and Allianz be the heirs of the Jewish families who were annihilated?

I raise this for another reason. As you surely recall, to defeat our efforts going back to 2007 in Congress to restore survivors' legal rights, the insurers, the State Department, and even some Jewish groups made the argument that restoring survivors' legal rights would result in less funding from Germany for the needs of indigent survivors. This was and is an outrageous argument. One thing has nothing to do with the other. Insurance companies should pay their debts and survivors should be able to sue them if they breach their contracts. That has nothing to do with *Germany's* long overdue moral obligation to provide adequate funding for the needs of survivors, a duty it has ignored and only recently began to address due to pressure from the survivors and our allies here in Congress.

But if you go back to the actual hearing record in the Senate back to 2007 and 2008, you will see that the Claims Conference witness cited this argument while was bragging about having secured $70 million from Germany for "additional home care funding" – for the entire world! We pointed out that $70 million for two years, or $35 million per year, for the 50,000 survivors then being served, would generate a total of $700 per survivor for home care funding – about 4 weeks of home care given the average cost of $15 and average need of 15 hours per week.

Germany doubled these home care funds again in 2010 and 2013, culminating in the home care fund discussed above that will address only 25% of the survivors' needs. If the funds from Germany have doubled three times and now will only meet one-quarter of the needs, this Committee can easily see that a far more direct and forceful response is desperately needed. This is what survivors are hoping will result from today's hearing and your next steps.

Of course, we hope and expect that Congress will take up a bill like HR 890 early next year and pass it so survivors can recover our family insurance policies. However, in addition, we believe that the insurers such as Allianz and Generali and others who profited from the Holocaust should also contribute to the kind of fund we are urging here to provide for all survivors' needs, immediately, and without further haggling. They have the money – they stole it. They can pay it out today to relieve survivors' suffering, some of which they caused.

Survivors' Care Remains Germany's Responsibility

Nothing has changed since Chancellor Adenauer's remarkable assertions of German responsibility in the 1950's! Instead Germany, under the present newly re-elected government has actively successfully pushed their own responsibilities to the US government and the American Jewish community instead. How bizarre is that? We are outraged and we beg this committee, especially you, Madame Chairwoman and Ranking Member Deutch, who have sat so ably on the Foreign Affairs Committee for all these years, to press the Secretary of State and the President, who have developed close ties to Chancellor Merkel and visited the camps with her and with Elie Wiesel, to change all this now, and get back to providing sufficient funds directly to meet survivors' actual physical and mental needs.

The cost of a proper, comprehensive, and permanent program would be minimal compared to Germany's and the insurers' resources – but would provide a vital lifeline to survivors who need and deserve it.

While you may think a turn-around is impossible to refocus on Germany's responsibility. We believe because of the very personal ties which exist uniquely at this time in the relationships with Chancellor Merkel, and with you, Madame Chairman, and the Secretary of State, a concerted effort to renew and refresh German's role is promising and should be tried on a concerted high level it should work. I am sure Elie Wiesel would join such an effort just as he did a the Prague conference on this subject and his visits with the President and Merkel at Bergen Belsen Concentration Camp as well as other such meetings.

Let me remind the Committee of Elie Wiesel's words to the 2009 Prague Conference:

> However, it is with pained sincerity that I must declare my conviction that living survivors of poor health or financial means, deserve first priority. They suffered enough. And enough people benefitted FROM their suffering. Why not do everything possible and draw from all available funds to help them live their last years with a sense of security, in dignity and serenity. All other parties can and must wait. Do not tell me that it ought to be the natural task of local Jewish communities; let's not discharge our responsibilities by placing them on their shoulders. WE have the funds. Let's use them for those survivors in our midst who are on the threshold of despair.

If only this could be the serious focus by all high level persons, led by you, Chairwoman Ros-Lehtinen and Ranking Member Deutch, it would finally cut through the talk and false efforts once and for all then to provide actual meaningful care not gimmicks which won't work once again leaving survivors continuing to suffer until they die.

Thank you again to the entire leadership of this Committee and Subcommittees to hear us, to bring these issues to light, and for your efforts past and future. They are historic and extremely important.

Ms. Ros-Lehtinen. Thank you, Mr. Rubin.

And I do notice that you cite here various testimony. And subject to the length limitation of the rules, we will try to put some of that testimony in the official part of the record. So I note your request.

Mrs. Firestone.

STATEMENT OF MS. KLARA FIRESTONE (DAUGHTER OF HOLOCAUST SURVIVORS)

Ms. Firestone. Thank you, Madam Chairman, for this rare opportunity to present. My name is Klara Firestone. I was born in Prague, Czechoslovakia, immediately following the end of World War II. And I am the daughter of two Holocaust survivors. I am the founder and president of Second Generation of Los Angeles. And I am also a psychotherapist, specializing in treating children of survivors.

Since 1978, I have been steeped in the Holocaust affairs, and have worked hand in glove with members of the survivor community in Los Angeles and our surrounding counties. I come here today to speak on behalf of myself, my family, and hundreds of survivors and second generation, who I have counseled and ministered to over the past 37 years and who have not had a voice to advocate for their rights. I have facilitated hundreds of support and therapy groups for children of all Holocaust survivors. And I have also been instrumental in helping survivor families navigate what have often been very complex and difficult relationships between parents and children, given the extreme trauma that served as the backdrop for our developmental years and most of our lives.

There is a long trail of problems that thousands of survivors and family members have confronted, too often with incredibly frustrating and painful outcomes. If half of all survivors worldwide, including in the United States, are living today in or near poverty, lacking the basics for a dignified old age, then the approach of the past 50 years is obviously wrong. I echo the words of others who have discussed the medical and emotional issues that survivors and the second generation must deal with on a daily basis. The problems are real, and they require serious, professional attention with properly trained health care and psychological caregivers who understand the unique problems that survivors and their children must deal with. Proper care requires a sea change in the funding available. And it is only just and right that this responsibility be assumed by the German Government and other entities that collaborated and profited from the Holocaust.

When the Holocaust ended, the fragments of Europe's Jewish communities emerged broken and tattered, wanting nothing more than to find who of their families survived and begin rebuilding their lives. They were too busy fighting their demons to care about fighting the bureaucracy in order to claim what was due to them. Many believed, as my mother also did then, that this was blood money. How can you compensate me for the loss of my parents, my brothers, my sisters, my aunts, my uncles, in dollars? What value should I assign that? So, once again, their claims and needs went unmet.

As the most active and visible leaders in our survivor community, my mother and I have been approached hundreds of times by

survivors and their children beseeching us to intervene on their behalf to recover restitution which is rightfully theirs. Time and
again we have attempted to do just that, and we too have met the
brick wall.

Even advocating for my own family has proved to no avail. My
beloved father passed away in 2001. Prior to his death, he had received a letter from the Claims Conference confirming that they
had assigned him a claim number for a particular fund, and he
would soon be receiving the moneys. After contacting them numerous times over the years, we are still waiting for those funds. They
now claim they are unable to find his claim in the system.

You cannot imagine the pain and frustration this causes the
loved ones of Holocaust survivors, not to mention re-traumatizing
the survivors themselves. And this is the kind of problem I hear
about over and over again.

Most importantly, I wish to touch on an issue which has not been
discussed before today, which is vitally urgent and which has no
other platform to be heard. That is the plight and suffering of
many of our second generation members, the forgotten victims of
the Nazi atrocities. There is an awareness now of something called
transmitted trauma, the concept that the trauma our parents went
through has been passed down to us, and the results of which
manifest as if they themselves had experienced the trauma directly, a sort of vicarious PTSD. I can't tell you the number of desperate calls I have received from survivor parents troubled over
their child's mental health. Some of the children have been so damaged by their teenage years that they have been totally dysfunctional the rest of their lives.

Dear committee members, we are at the eleventh hour and 59
minutes. And if something is not done quickly and sufficiently, my
fear is that thousands of the remaining survivors will die tragically
suffering their unmet medical and psychological needs. You called
this hearing to see what can be done today to remedy this dire situation. And the answer is plain: Simply put, Germany must fulfill
its moral responsibility to care for all the medical and mental
health needs of the survivors and their families, with no more
shifting of these huge responsibilities onto the shoulders of others
who had no hand in creating these conditions. If this committee
does only one thing as a result of this hearing, it should be a concerted, bipartisan, and relentless effort to convince Chancellor
Merkel and the German Bundestag to make good on Chancellor
Adenauer's pledge in 1952 to take care of Holocaust survivors "to
their last breath" and to fully fund the needs of our aging survivors
without offset or delay. In addition, we would strongly urge that a
new vehicle for distribution of these funds be required, with full
transparency and oversight.

I thank Chairman Ros-Lehtinen for allowing me to testify today.

I am particularly gratified that Chairman Rohrabacher, who is
from my State, has agreed to cochair.

I thank the ranking member, Congressman Deutch, who along
with Congresswoman Ros-Lehtinen, have been our steadfast champions.

It is heartfelt. You don't know.

31

And I ask that certain exhibits be allowed to be also entered into the record.

Ms. ROS-LEHTINEN. Without objection, subject to the length limitation and rules.

Thank you very much for powerful testimony, Mrs. Firestone.

[The prepared statement of Ms. Firestone was received after the hearing and appears in the appendix.]

Ms. ROS-LEHTINEN. Dr. Paris. Thank you.

STATEMENT OF BARBARA PARIS, M.D. (PHYSICIAN WHO FOCUSES ON THE CARE OF HOLOCAUST SURVIVORS)

Dr. PARIS. Good afternoon, Chair Ros-Lehtinen, ranking committee members and subcommittee members. I am very grateful for the opportunity to speak before all of you today.

Echoing in my head all day all the time is, ''Doctor, I can't sleep because every time I close my eyes, I am in Auschwitz.'' How can I take care of this patient, a demented, elderly woman? Every time I visit her at home she is exhausted and she just can't even close her eyes, telling me how she is so fearful of doing that.

Can you, committee members and members of the audience, imagine the trauma of a child, a teenager, a parent being brutally shoved into a cattle car with no air, no bathroom, no food, for days. And that was just the beginning. Lined up for hours in the bitter cold with no shoes or coats, shaved heads, smelling the burning bodies and their loved ones in the crematoria.

I ask you, committee members, does the German Government really need to spend their money interviewing anyone who could possibly have survived Hitler's dehumanization, torture, rape, medical experiments, starvation, and death marches? Do they really need to interview the few people who have survived to determined if they have been psychologically and physically harmed enough to deserve reparations? It seems absurd to me.

Even when the German psychiatrist acknowledges damage, these patients are not physically or emotionally capable of completing the highly formalistic, complicated, and overly bureaucratic correspondence requiring yearly physician input, notarization, and more. I as a physician, with all of my degrees, am truly challenged to complete these forms. They are written in German, and they ask for a level of detail about past events that I cannot ascertain from a demented patient. And from other patients, it is very traumatizing to have to relive these details and be forced to rejustify their right to reparations every single year. It is a very clever way of withholding money from disabled people.

Thankfully, many survivors are well into their 90s, and I have the honor and privilege to be their doctor. While they have exhibited tremendous vitality in building new lives and families in America, they have sublimated their losses into flawed parent-child relationships, night terrors, and silently reliving the Holocaust in a hell to themselves. One second generation survivor poignantly pointed out to me, although I did not realize this as a child, I understand now that the Holocaust was playing out in my living room every single day.

Make no mistake, every survivor suffers from post-traumatic stress disorder. The German Government needs to face this crystal clear fact and begin to act upon it. I just want to review what exactly this means, post-traumatic stress disorder. It is a disorder that occurs when a person has experienced, witnessed, or was confronted with an event that involved actual or threatened death or serious injury, or a threat to the physical integrity of self or others. And the person's response involved intense fear, helplessness, or horror. It is characterized by repeated reliving of the life-threatening events in the form of images, thoughts, illusions, flashbacks, dreams, or hallucinations. I wonder how many health care providers today actually make that connection with a patient in front of them.

A close professional colleague, Jochanan Stessman, has been studying aging survivors in Jerusalem since 1990 and comparing them to nonsurvivors of the same age residing in Jerusalem. Survivors tend to be less educated, have fewer social supports, greater difficulties with activities of daily living, and greater uses of psychiatric medications. This, of course, is not surprising and must be addressed. Aging survivors, with more time on their hands and fewer activities to occupy their day, are back in the ghettoes and concentration camps, grieving for their dead relatives, hiding food in their beds, depressed and guilt ridden that they survived, afraid of doctors, fearing to acknowledge any weakness, as that was an automatic death sentence, anxious about showers, standing on lines, wearing I.D. bracelets, and lots more.

We need resources to create comforting, affordable care home environments designed that do not trigger these fears in these people. In their retirement and facing death of spouses and friends, survivors are beginning to uncover these painful, suppressed memories, and grieve the deaths of their own parents, sisters, brothers and, in many cases, their own children. For these survivors, the year is 1946; it is not 2014. Doctors and other health care providers and caregivers are not educated in the unique skill sets needed to respectfully and compassionately help survivors live in their final years in relative peace. Caring for survivors requires fully trained health care professionals who understand this unique population's emotional and medical needs.

And what about their children, the second generation, and even the third generation? Their therapists, mostly, don't understand this transgenerational effect of trauma on their own emotional difficulties, including failed interpersonal relationships, depression, anxiety, schizophrenia, and much more. Their parents, depleted of psychological resources, were often emotionally detached but simultaneously feared any separation from their children in very suffocating ways. One frustrated lawyer son of survivors tells me the reparations program totally ignores emotional mental scarring and financial needs of the offspring of survivors. Growing up in a home with a parent who was incapable of nurturing her children led me to many years of psychotherapy. Yet the Germans refuse to acknowledge any causal connection or obligation to reimburse my therapy expenses. In fact, they exhibit a rigid, myopic notion that insisted that the effects of the Holocaust were not passed onto the children of survivors. Or even if there was some leakage, Germany maintains it has no obligation to compensate or assist members of that select offspring group.

I ask you, committee members, how much can the recently announced $3,280 cover in expenses for child survivors? A set of dentures? A set of hearing aids? Six weeks of a 24-hour home attendant? How many home visits with an occupational therapist, a medical doctor, psychiatrist, social worker, bereavement counselor, medications? One month's rent? Transportation costs? It does not even make a dent in addressing the ongoing, unmet medical and psychosocial needs.

AMCHA, the National Center for Psychosocial Support of Survivors of the Holocaust and the Second Generation, is a group in Israel that has developed a rich body of unique knowledge in the late effects of Holocaust traumatization and its intergenerational transmission. You have an article that I submitted that tells you about the needed resources. The financial needs for caring, the resources, and education of caregivers and health providers are many. We must advocate for our citizens here who came here physically and emotionally spent, yet managed to rebuild their lives at great personal cost. We must not ignore or minimize their needs and the needs of their offspring. I am honored to have this opportunity to spell this out to you in Congress. And this is only a small part of what I do all day. I struggle daily to creatively piecemeal together and coordinate all the far too few resources that can help provide a modicum of relief and maybe even a little pleasure to these survivors in the last years of their lives. Their families are running out of time, as you have heard. They are depending on this committee and Congress to step in and use your power to help them and to be responsible in providing the many, many unmet needs of this population and their offspring. Thank you.

Ms. ROS-LEHTINEN. Thank you very much for very vivid testimony about the real effects.

[The prepared statement of Dr. Paris follows:]

House Foreign Affairs Committee
Hearing on Holocaust Survivor Care Needs
September 18, 2014

Prepared and Submitted by Barbara Paris, MD

Chairman Ros-Lehtinen, Ranking Member Deutch and members of the subcommittee.

I am grateful for the opportunity to speak before you today.

" Doctor, I cannot sleep because every time I close my eyes, I am in Auschwitz". During each home visit to my demented elderly patient those were her words. I cannot get them out of my head.

Can you, Committee members, imagine the trauma of a child, a teenager, a parent being brutally shoved into a cattle car, with no air, no bathroom and no food for days? At that was just the beginning. Lined up for hours in the bitter cold with no shoes or coats, shaved heads, smelling the burning bodies of there loved in the crematoria.

I am privileged, as a physician whose career has been devoted to caring for survivors and their family members, to provide a few important observations. Time does not permit me to adequately address the multitude of obstacles that currently prevent Holocaust survivors from receiving the resources and care they need for dignity in their final years. By this I refer to everything from the simple failure of Germany to acknowledge and commit to providing to address all survivors' physical and emotional needs, to the horrific maze of opaque guidelines and ludicrous paperwork demands and deadlines imposed by Germany and the Claims Conference in various programs.

Does the German Government really need to spend their money interviewing anyone who could possibly survive Hitler's dehumanization, torture, rape, medical experiments, starvation and death marches to determine if they have been psychologically and physically harmed enough to deserve reparations? Even when the German psychiatrist acknowledges damage, these patients are not physically or emotionally capable of completing highly formalistic, complicated and overly bureaucratic correspondence requiring yearly physician input, notarization and more. As a physician, I am challenged to complete forms written in German and asking for a level of detail about past events that I cannot ascertain from a demented patient and for other patients it is traumatizing to have to relive these details and be forced to " re-justify" their right to reparations every year. It is a clever way of withholding money from disabled people.

Thankfully, many survivors are well in their nineties and I have the honor and the privilege to be their doctor. While they have exhibited tremendous vitality in building new lives and families in America, they sublimated their losses into flawed parent - child relationships, night terrors, and silently replayed their living hell to themselves. One second generation survivor poignantly told me, "although I did not realize this a child, I understand now that the holocaust was playing out in our living room everyday." Make no mistake, every survivor suffers from PTSD. The German government needs to face this crystal clear fact and act upon it."

 The medical definition of PTSD is as follows;

A disorder that occurs when a person has 'experienced, witnessed, or was confronted with an event that involved actual or threatened death or serious injury, or a threat to the physical integrity of self or others," and " the person's response involved intense fear, helplessness, or horror." It is characterized by repeated reliving of the life-threatening events in the form of images, thoughts, illusions, flashbacks, dreams or hallucinations.

A close professional colleague has been studying aging survivors in Jerusalem since 1990 and comparing them to non-survivors of the same age residing in Jerusalem. Survivors are less educated, have fewer social supports, greater difficulties with activities of daily living and greater usage of psychiatric medications. This is not surprising and must be addressed. Aging survivors, with time and fewer activities to occupy their day are back in the ghettos and concentration camps, grieving for their dead relatives, hiding food in their beds, depressed that they survived, afraid of doctors, fearful of acknowledging weakness (that was an automatic death sentence) anxious about showers, standing on line, wearing ID bracelets and lots more.

We need resources to manage them in comforting environments designed NOT to trigger these fears. Only now, in their retirement, and facing death of spouses and friends are they beginning to uncover these painful suppressed memories and grieve the death of their own parents, sisters and brothers. For these survivors the year is 1946, not 2014. All Doctors and other health care providers and caregivers are not educated in the unique skill sets needed to respectfully and compassionately help survivors live their final year in relative peace. Caring for survivors really requires fully trained health care professionals who understand this unique population's emotional and medical needs. Well-intended but not well-informed or funded programs that give the appearance of assistance really just divert attention from the vast gulf that exists between survivors' needs and available resources and programs.

What about their children? Most second-generation survivors and their therapists do not understand this trans-generational effect of trauma on their own emotional difficulties including failed interpersonal relationships, depression, and anxiety. Schizophrenia and much more. Their parents, depleted of psychological resources, were often emotionally detached but simultaneously feared any separation from their children in suffocating ways.

One frustrated, lawyer son of survivors tells me" the reparations program totally ignores emotional/mental scarring and financial needs of the offspring of survivors. Growing up in a home with a parent who was incapable of nurturing her children, led me to many years of psychotherapy- yet the Germans refuse to acknowledge any causal connection or obligation to reimburse my therapy expenses. In fact, they exhibited a rigid myopic notion that insisted that the effects of the Holocaust were not passed on to children of survivors, or even if there was some "leakage", Germany maintains that it has no obligation to compensate or assist members of that "select" offspring group.

I am continuously frustrated and bewildered by grandiose announcements from Germany and the Claims Conference concerning new benefit programs. Have they ever taken a measure of the full scope of the needs and simply decided that Germany will now and going forward pay what is needed? Why not? This applies to last year's home care fund announcement, which will fall far short of meeting the actual home care needs of survivors, as well as this month's announcement for child survivors.

I ask you, committee members, how much can $3280 cover in expenses for child survivors?

I set of dentures? I set of hearing aides? Six weeks of a 24-hour home attendant? Home visits with an occupational therapist, a medical doctor, psychiatrist or social worker? Bereavement counseling? Medication costs? Transportation costs? It does not even make a dent in addressing their medical and psychological needs. AMCHA, the National Center for Psychosocial Support of Survivors of the Holocaust and the Second Generation has developed a rich body of unique knowledge in the late effects of Holocaust traumatization an its intergenerational transmission. Resources are needed to implement the wide range of therapies that AMCHA has been utilizing to treat these victims.

The financial needs for care, resources, and education of caregivers and health care providers are many. We must advocate for our citizens who came here physically and emotionally spent, yet managed to rebuild their lives at great personal cost. We must not ignore or minimize their needs and the needs of their offspring. I am very honored to have this opportunity to spell out for the Congress a small part of what the problem is. I struggle daily to creatively piecemeal together and coordinate the far too few resources that can help provide a modicum of relief. The survivors and their families are running out of time, truly. They are depending on this Committee and Congress to step in where others have failed, and use your powers as the elected officials of our country to demand that Germany and other responsible institutions step up and finally do what is morally necessary. You have the power to help. Thank you.

Ms. ROS-LEHTINEN. Did you want that article to be included as part of the record?

Dr. PARIS. Yes.

Ms. ROS-LEHTINEN. Without objection, and subject to the length limitation in the rules.

Thank you, Dr. Paris.

Ms. Lieberman.

STATEMENT OF MS. EUGENIE LIEBERMAN (DAUGHTER OF HOLOCAUST SURVIVOR)

Ms. LIEBERMAN. Madam Chairperson and committee members, thank you for giving me the opportunity to speak with you here today. And before I start my prepared statement, I just want to say that the testimony of the other witnesses resonated very profoundly with me, especially the last of Dr. Paris.

So, to begin, my name, as you know, is Eugenie Lieberman. I was born Eugenie Segalowitz, the daughter of Ivar Segalowitz, who some of you may have met before. Ivar was a Holocaust survivors who lived and raised his family in Great Neck, New York. Sadly, my father passed away just a few months ago, succumbing to prostate cancer on June 23rd, 2014.

My mother, Bernie Segalowitz, who still resides in Great Neck; my brother, Ralph Segalowitz, who lives in East Setauket, Long Island; our children, Suzanne, Melissa, Jonathan, and Michael; spouses, Cathy and Jay; and I, will carry on his legacy of fighting for the rights of survivors. The sense of purpose and dedication to humanitarian causes that my father instilled in us brings me here today. My father was born in Memel/Klaipeda, Lithuania, on August 17—1930, of parents who were German citizens. The entire family—his parents, Erna and Boris; his aunt Anna; and Aunt Eugenie, after whom I am named; Uncle Tobias Mazur; his grandmother; and great aunt, were all killed by the Nazis. Ivar, my father, survived life in three concentration camps, having endured imprisonment in the Kovno Ghetto, then Dachau, Auschwitz/Birkenau, and, finally, a death march to Buchenwald. At 14 years of age, on April 11, 1945, he was liberated from Buchenwald by the American Army. He was the only member of his incarcerated family to survive. Upon liberation, he was shipped to a school for orphaned children of the Holocaust in France. And after being there for 2 years, his aunt, his mother's sister, who had come to the United States before World War II, found him with the help of the Red Cross and brought him—sponsored him to come to this country.

When he got to the United States, he finished his high school education by attending Stuyvesant High School at night and obtained vocational training as a machinist during the day. In the following years, he worked in machine shops, began attending college at night, got married, served in the United States Army Intelligence Corps as a corporal during the Korean Conflict.

In 1968, he graduated from City College of New York with a bachelor's degree in physics. My father spent most of his working career in manufacturing, serving as VP for two companies on Long Island and then as a consultant, obtaining six patents by the end of his time in the public sector. In 2002, he was elected for his first

3-year term as a Great Neck parks commissioner. He served in that capacity for three consecutive terms, making significant contributions to the community, for a total of 9 years.

Before World War II, Ivar's father, my grandfather, Boris, was a successful processor and distributor of flax products in Lithuania. Ivar's grandmother owned a popular shoe store. My father always believed that his father would have provided for his offspring with life insurance. He knows that both his father and grandmother were responsible business people who were committed to their families. They would have purchased insurance in good faith. My father, the only member of his family to survive the Holocaust, a U.S. military and Korean War veteran and a former elected official on Long Island, was also heir to several insurance policies, likely sold to his family by European life insurance companies. Yet after all this service and participation in American civic life, he was unable to employ the basic constitutional rights to bring suit on the insurance companies in court.

For as many years as I can remember, my father was active in pressing for all survivors to have their insurance rights restored and to find help for tens of thousands of Holocaust survivors living in poverty. He was on the executive committee of the Holocaust Survivors Foundation and had traveled to Washington on several occasions to lobby the New York congressional delegation on these issues.

My father was anguished and disappointed by the fact that the United States Government he revered and served would oppose his basic right to go to court to pursue his family's insurance policies. He knew he might not win, but how could he not even have the right to try? He could not understand how Congress repeatedly turned the survivors down.

I cannot understand that my father, a giant in life, died despite the incredible losses he endured, without the ability under U.S. law to reclaim the legacies of his parents, his grandparents, and other relatives, and that he was one of thousands, many of whom already died in frustration, whose rights had been denied as well.

Now Ivar is gone and will never have the satisfaction of learning about this part of his family's history, even though the records exist. Ivar had spent an extensive amount of time and effort compiling information to support his claims. He had presented these documents and information to the proper organizations, institutions, and governmental agencies, with no satisfactory response. We only ask your assistance in obtaining the definitive proof that these policies existed and providing the judicial forum in which to obligate the companies to disburse the benefits to the insureds' legal beneficiaries and heirs.

Ivar submitted claims to the ICHEIC on his relatives who were listed on the Web site. The only policy that was acknowledged was for Siegmund Joseph, his grandfather, who died in 1929 and whose policy was paid out. ICHEIC couldn't find any information about the other relatives whose names were published, who were all alive when the Holocaust began.

Recently, I attempted to meet with the German consulate in Miami about these issues and was left disregarded in the waiting room for 2½ hours with an appointment.

The unpaid policies have remained secret and not accessible to Ivar or his children despite the fact that German insurers published his relatives' names on the ICHEIC Web site, proving that these individuals did have policies. But the system has denied him all this information, including the names of the companies who sold the policies.

My father also devoted many hours in his retirement advocating for the needs of indigent survivors who could not afford the basic necessities for a dignified old age. Thankfully, my father's situation was such that he could obtain the care he needed. But he knew that so many other survivors were not so lucky. He saw firsthand the prisoners subjected to unimaginable physical and emotional injuries at the hands of the Nazi regime.

If he were here today, he would urge Congress to use its influence with the German Government and companies that profited from the Holocaust to provide full funding for the needs of Holocaust survivors who need help throughout the world.

Madam Chairman and members, thank you for allowing me to testify.

And please include the attached exhibits in the record of the hearing.

Ms. ROS-LEHTINEN. Without objection, subject to the length limitation of the rules.

[The prepared statement of Ms. Lieberman follows:]

Statement of Eugenie Lieberman
United States House of Representatives
Committee on Foreign Affairs
The Struggles of Recovering Assets for Holocaust Survivors
September 18, 2014

My name is Eugenie Lieberman, born Eugenie Segalowitz, daughter of Ivar Segalowitz. Ivar was a Holocaust survivor who lived and raised his family in Great Neck, New York. Sadly, my father passed away just a few months ago, succumbing to Prostate Cancer on June 23, 2014. My mother, Bernice Segalowitz, who still resides in Great Neck, my brother, Ralph Segalowitz, who lives in East Setauket, LI, our children, Suzanne, Melissa, Jonathon, and Michael, spouses, Cathy and Jay, and I will carry on his legacy of fighting for the rights of survivors. The sense of purpose and dedication to humanitarian causes that my father instilled in us brings me here today.

My father was born in Memel/Klaipeda Lithuania on August 17, 1930 of parents who were German citizens. The entire family, parents, Erna and Boris, Aunt Eugenie (after whom I am named), Uncle Tobias Mazur, his grandmother and great aunt, were all killed by the Nazi's. Ivar survived life in three concentration camps, having endured imprisonment in the Kovno Ghetto, then Dachau, Auschwitz/ Birkenau, and finally a death march to Buchenwald. At fourteen years of age, on April 11, 1945, he was liberated from Buchenwald by the American Army. He was the only member of his incarcerated family to survive. Upon liberation, he was shipped to a school for orphaned children of the Holocaust in France. After being there for two years, his aunt, his mother's sister, who had come to the United States before WWII, found him with the help of the Red Cross and sponsored him to come to this country.

When he got to the United States, he finished his high school education by attending Stuyvesant High School at night and obtained vocational training as a machinist during the day. In the following years, he worked in machine shops, began attending college at night, got married and served in the United States Army Intelligence Corp as a corporal during the Korean conflict. In 1968, he graduated from the City College of NY with a Bachelor's degree in Physics.

My father spent most of his working career in manufacturing engineering, serving as VP of Manufacturing for two companies on Long Island, and then as a consultant, obtaining 6 patents by the end of his time in the public sector.

In 2002, he was elected for his first three year term as a Great Neck Parks Commissioner. He served in that capacity for three consecutive terms, making significant contributions to the community, for a total of nine years.

Before World War II, Ivar's father, Boris, was a successful processor and distributor of Flax products in Lithuania. Ivar's grandmother owned a popular shoe store. My father always believed that his father would have provided for his offspring with Life Insurance. He knows that his father and grandmother were responsible business people, who were committed to their families. They would have purchased insurance in good faith.

My father, Ivar Segalowitz, survived several camps and death marches and was the only member of his family to survive the Holocaust. He was a U.S. military and Korean War veteran and a former elected official on Long Island. He was also the heir to several insurance policies – likely sold by European life insurance companies. Yet after all this service and participation in American civic life, he was unable to employ the basic constitutional right to sue insurance companies who cheated his family.

For as many years as I can remember, my father was active in pressing for all survivors to have their insurance rights restored, and to find help for the tens of thousands of Holocaust survivors living in poverty. He was on the Executive Committee of the Holocaust Survivors Foundation, and had traveled to Washington, D.C. on several occasions to lobby the New York Congressional delegation on these issues. He also reached out, on numerous occasions, to New York House Members and Senators to no avail.

My father was tortured by the fact that the United States government he revered and served would oppose his having the basic right to go to Court to pursue his family's insurance policies. This was tragically the case under both Presidents Bush and Obama. He knew he might not win, but how could he not even have the right to have a judge and jury of his peers hear his case?

He could not understand how Congress repeatedly turned the survivors down. In December 2013, even as he battled with his cancer that was growing more serious, my father left his sick bed to come into Manhattan to join a protest with other survivors when a Jewish organization was holding a dinner to honor the lobbyist for one of the major European insurance companies.

It is unfathomable to me at this point that this giant in life died as a second class citizen under U.S. law, despite the incredible losses he endured, and without the ability to reclaim the legacies of his parents, grandparents, and other relatives. After all, he was at the time one of thousands – many of whom have already died in frustration and humiliation, whose humanity has been denied by their own government.

Now Ivar is gone and will never have the satisfaction of learning about this part of his family's history – even though the records exist.

Ivar Segalowitz Insurance Claims

Ivar had spent an extensive amount of time and effort compiling information to support his claims. He had presented these documents and information to the proper organizations, institutions, and governmental agencies with no satisfactory response. From the available evidence, we can draw the conclusion that it was the intent of our relatives to purchase and keep their policies in force until they were needed. We only ask your assistance in obtaining the definitive proof that these policies existed and providing the judicial forum in which to obligate the companies to disburse the benefits to the insured's legal beneficiaries and heirs.

Ivar submitted claims to the International Commission for Holocaust Era Insurance Claims (ICHEIC) on the following relatives whose names were listed on the ICHEIC website:

Erna Segalowitz his mother

Siegmund Joseph, his maternal grandfather

Minna (Benjamin) Joseph, is maternal grandmother

Walter Lephene (Lepane) – Uncle, Mother's sister's husband

Margot (Joseph) Lephene (Lepane) – Aunt, Mother's sister

The <u>only</u> policy that was acknowledged was for Siegmund Joseph, his grandfather, who died in 1929 and whose policy was paid out.   His name was on the list published. However, as to the other four relatives whose names were published, who all were alive when the Holocaust began, ICHEIC "couldn't find" any information about any of them.

In other words the only one that these companies "found" was the one that was already paid, so there was no harm in giving him that information. However, the unpaid policies remain secret and not accessible to Ivar despite the fact that the German insurers published his relatives' names on the ICHEIC website, proving that these individuals did have policies.   But the system has simply denied him all information, including the names of the companies that sold the policies!   (ICHEIC sent Ivar $1000 as a "humanitarian payment.")

This was part of ICHEIC's deal with Germany – names were published but the identity of the companies remained secret.   That is ridiculous. And since Ivar was a Holocaust survivor, he does not have the right to go to court to get this information from Allianz, the most prominent German insurer of the time, or the German Insurance Association, which placed the names on the ICHEIC website.   There is no legal remedy for him due to the U.S. government's court filings and the failure of Congress to act. As my father would have, I am asking that the leaders of this Congress introduce and pass legislation restoring survivors' insurance rights, like the legislation that was blocked in 2012, as soon as you can in 2015.

<u>Needs of Indigent Holocaust Survivors</u>

My father also devoted many hours in his retirement years advocating for the needs of indigent survivors who could not afford the basic necessities for a dignified old age. Thankfully, my father's financial situation was such that he could obtain the care he needed. But he knew that so many other survivors were not so lucky. He understood how many survivors suffered from unimaginable physical and emotional injuries they suffered at the hands of the Nazi regime.   If he were here today, he would also urge Congress to use its influence with the German government and other companies and countries that profited from the Holocaust to provide full funding for the needs of Holocaust survivors who need help throughout the world.

_____

Ms. ROS-LEHTINEN. Ivar would be very proud to see you continuing the fight. Thank you very much.

Thank you to all of our witnesses. Our panel has been extraordinary. Thank you for your courage. Thank you for your strength to keep at this year in and year out and never giving up. For everything you have done and will continue to do on behalf of Holocaust survivors in the U.S., Israel, worldwide, this hearing is about the needs and the well-being of survivors and their families.

Regretfully, nearly 70 years later, humanity continues to fail the victims of Hitler and the Nazis. We have heard your heartbreaking and remarkable stories. And, again, I just want to say how truly inspiring each and every one of you is. As I said, my constituents continue to tell me about the failures of not just the other governments, but sadly, our own great, terrific government has let them down as well. My good friends David Mermelstein and his wife, Irene; Joe Sachs and his wife, Marcia; David Schachter; Alex Gross; Alex Moskowitz; Herb Karliner, so many others. They repeatedly tell me that they feel let down by our efforts on behalf of survivors.

So, Mr. Rubin and Ms. Firestone, two questions for you. What more can we do in Congress? What more can our U.S. Government do to help alleviate some of these concerns? Also, what challenges and obstacles do survivors continue to face? And Dr. Paris, I would like to ask you a question. You have dedicated most of your career to the care of Holocaust survivors and their families. You detailed so many concerns that they have. What are the most common health issues that impact survivors? How can we help to ensure that they are getting the proper care and treatment that they need?

And that first question for Mr. Rubin, Ms. Firestone, is also for you, Ms. Lieberman, because the second generation of survivors.

And Ms. Firestone, you work with heirs and families of survivors. I think a lot of the times we overlook the toll that is taken on the families, the children of survivors, the many issues that they face. How are the problems facing the second generation different from the survivors? And do we have programs currently out there that can address those issues? So a lot of questions.

We will begin with you, Mr. Rubin.

Mr. RUBIN. Well, like I said before, Nazi Germany caused this problem that we are having today. And I think the German Government should be responsible to see to it that those of us who are still alive, that we can live out our lives in dignity, not in misery. I myself am very fortunate. I worked very hard. Thank God, I don't have to go on welfare. But a lot of people, a lot of Holocaust survivors, they don't have the same pleasant situation. And, like I said, Congress could see to it that the German Government sees to it, like Chancellor Adenauer promised, that Germany will take care of the Holocaust survivors to their last breath. So I don't know, Germany does not honor their Chancellor, and that is a shame, because that was his request when he became Chancellor of a democratic Germany. And Germany could afford it.

Not only Germany, but also the insurance companies who robbed us, robbed our parents' policies. And they are sitting on billions of dollars. They are holding onto it. And they don't even want to see to it that they just help us a little bit so we should have some final answers to see to it that those Holocaust survivors who are in need should be getting it. Thank you.

Ms. ROS-LEHTINEN. Thank you, Mr. Rubin.

Ms. Firestone.

Ms. FIRESTONE. Thank you. I think that what people don't realize is the vastness of the Holocaust, the far-reaching effects of the Holocaust. The ripple effects go down not only to the second generation, but the third and sometimes the fourth generation. But the second generation is very, very unique among populations, especially for mental health.

And if I might just point out a couple of things briefly. Number one, we are a generation, if you can imagine, totally cut off from our ancestry. The buck stopped here at the Holocaust. We stand in the same position almost as an adopted child who doesn't know where they came from. We begin at day one after the Holocaust. And we have no extended families, had no extended families, or only fragments of extended families to raise us and support us, where others had grandparents and aunts and uncles and cousins for whom they could rely on support, especially emotionally.

Because we had parents raising us who were children themselves when they went through the Holocaust and who had no training in parenting. So when they, in desperation, coupled up after the war, they now went on to raise children. With what tools? With what emotional tools? They didn't have them. So we, the second generation, really got the brunt of it emotionally, because our parents up until the Holocaust had the benefit of wonderful childhoods up until that dire time in history.

So whatever can be done that brings funding for mental health for second generation, I am begging you, it needs to be done. We have survivors who come to me because their children have been totally disabled and dysfunctional their entire lives. And now they are coming to the end of their lives, and they are frightened about what will happen to their children who can't provide for themselves financially. And this is a very real concern and a very big concern. It is not just one or two people. So, again, whatever can be done.

Certainly Germany needs to provide the adequate funding. It was they who caused the problem. And they need to accept that responsibility and provide adequate funds for it. But the Claims Conference needs to get up off the money and start giving it to the people for whom it was negotiated.

Ms. ROS-LEHTINEN. If I could interrupt, because I know we have two more witnesses to answer. About the Claims Conference, about ICHEIC, so often we hear that this was settled, everything was taken care of, everyone signed forms, all the claims were paid out. And, in fact, very few claims were actually paid out. And one thing that ICHEIC was very successful in doing is denying you the right to go to court. What happens when a survivor puts in a claim in court and wants to have their day in court? What happens there?

Ms. FIRESTONE. Well, now they don't put it into court. There was a remainder committee created in New York that ostensibly is supposed to deal with those claims. And, yes, maybe a handful of claims have come through. My cousin was the first person to receive restitution from ICHEIC. Because at the very magical occurrence when he returned home after the war, he found the insurance policy of his parents. So he did have——

Ms. ROS-LEHTINEN. Which is very difficult for survivors and family members.

Ms. FIRESTONE. It is not difficult; the word is "impossible." No one marched off to Auschwitz with anything. And no one got to Auschwitz and 5 minutes later had anything—and certainly not documents. So this was the rarest of occurrences that he would have found this document still in the family home.

When his nephew went to claim, because the families had these insurance policies, he was told it had already been settled. He didn't even know that his uncle had claimed on the document. But why didn't they do due diligence? Why didn't they find out that there were other family members? Because they never put out adequate notices for us to know what was going on, for us to be able to come forward to do that.

The same thing happened with the German properties in East Germany. They gave a 2-year window. What kind of 2-year window is that for the world to find out about something if you are not putting out adequate notices for us to even know that we can do this? But even when we tried, we get the door slammed in our face all the time. And ICHEIC paid out all of 3 percent of the moneys and claimed that they did a great job.

The Claims Conference claims the same thing. They negotiated all these billions of dollars over the years, and they are still holding on to all of it. Why wasn't it just given in the claims to the survivors when they claimed it?

Ms. ROS-LEHTINEN. The mechanisms were there, but it was never successful. Yet they—because they existed, they are able to say, See, we had this, everybody is fine.

Ms. FIRESTONE. And in addition, the Claims Conference, and I know this from people who came to me for help, very often they had the proof of the claims, and they suffered the atrocities and the indignities, but artificial roadblocks were placed in there by the Claims Conference claiming that Germany had done it. Well, I have a friend in Germany who is an attorney. And I asked him at one point to please look into a particular case. He came back and told me there was no such roadblock given by the Germans. It was the Claims Conference who did it.

Ms. ROS-LEHTINEN. Thank you very much.

Dr. Paris and Ms. Lieberman.

Dr. PARIS. Thank you. Oftentimes, or when I am dealing with a patient that comes into my office, I am actually dealing a dyad, a mother-daughter, a mother-son, or the whole family of multiple children and the patient, as a geriatrician, is usually the older patient. But it doesn't really turn out that way because you really have to treat the whole family in order to treat the patient.

And I think that brings up family therapy as a very significant unmet need in taking care of survivors and their offspring. Because there are many roadblocks to the care of the patient because the children in their dysfunctional relationships with their parents often create roadblocks to the appropriate care on many levels. Very specific health care needs I think are well documented in the literature and you are familiar with. You mentioned osteoporosis, the consequences for my patients are severe compression fractures, severe pain, immobility, and severe degenerative joint disease, multiple replacement of joints because of severely worn out joints. Terrible problems with teeth and dentures, which have tremendous effect on the whole well-being of the person in terms of malnutrition as a result of that and even heart disease, endocarditis because of an infection from very poor gum care over many years.

It is important to point out that it is not a medical and a psychiatric need. Somebody who has post-traumatic stress disorder, severe anxiety, depression, paranoid behavior, that affects their physical health, too. So it is one sort of combined problem in these patients. It is frustrating for doctors, most of whom don't have the sensitivity or understanding of this. And they say, Here is a pill. And it doesn't work, and the family member doesn't give it, and the patient doesn't want to take it because they are so paranoid of all medical care that it becomes a very complex management team to even take care of what otherwise might be a very simple medical problem.

Ms. Ros-Lehtinen. Thank you.

Dr. Paris. I think it is very important to recognize that. And now many of the people that I am taking care of are well into their 90s. And we are into a whole host of new medical care needs that have to do with end-of-life issues. And often patients and their children are unable to let go. They are unable to see suffering in their parents. But yet, at the same time, my mother saw death; you need to do everything to keep her alive right now. And inappropriate treatments or painful treatments because they just can't let go. And doctors are not trained in how to sensitively discuss end-of-life issues and goals of care with these patients.

Ms. Ros-Lehtinen. Thank you, Dr. Paris. I am just so way out of time.

I want to give Ms. Lieberman a chance to answer. Thank you so much.

Ms. Lieberman. Okay. As a child of a Holocaust survivor, I think Dr. Paris explained some of the challenges that we deal with. And then, as a parent in this country in this time, you want to bring up your children to be productive and happy members of society. My husband and I are both children of Holocaust survivors. And every day we face the challenge and exert great effort to make sure that the effects and horror of our parents' broken childhood and their survivorship ends with us. And I am not sure we always do that successfully.

In terms of your question, what would be appreciated or what kind of programs would we like to see in the future, from my point of view—and I hope I am representative of other survivors—we would be grateful for any programs that would enable us to reach that goal that all of us as parents want for our children, not to suffer the consequences of us having parents who are Holocaust survivors and underwent the horrific situations that they went through.

And then, in terms of ICHEIC, I think the bottom line there is to have a legal remedy for citizens of the U.S. Government to file in the courts and be able to move the insurance companies forward with opening their books and allowing us to see who actually had insurance policies and who didn't.

Ms. ROS-LEHTINEN. What a concept. Thank you so much.

Thank you to all of our panelists.

So pleased to yield to another fighter for Holocaust survivors, Mr. Deutch, my colleague.

Mr. DEUTCH. Thank you, Madam Chairman.

And thanks to our witnesses today. I want to come at this a little bit differently. And I want to do it because of a conversation that Mr. Rubin and I had when I spoke with him as he was preparing his testimony before coming up here.

And he told me that—I believe what you said, Mr. Rubin, is, I am 86—86—I am tired, and I just can't keep doing this. We can— and this is as much to the witnesses as it is to every group who is paying attention to this hearing. And for all of the groups that were worried, quite frankly, about where this hearing might go, let me be clear: Mr. Rubin is right. It is time that we do the math, that we determine what doctors and professionals have mandated in order to address—I am quoting you—the physical and mental illnesses, in order to address the emotional needs, housing, home health care, dental care. Let's figure out what the needs are. And I am going to say something different. When I was in the State Senate, and now in Congress, we have worked to press insurance companies to open their books so that survivors can pursue justice, and I believe that.

But I want to be clear, this is not, nor should it become, an ongoing battle to defend actions that have taken place in the past. This should be an effort to focus on the fact that there are survivors who are old and dying and need help. And we don't need to attack—the groups don't need to attack one another. And let's just—let's assume good will on all sides. I acknowledge that, despite some of the accusations against the Claims Conference and its successor organization for mismanagement of funds, there are an enormous number of people who have devoted substantial amounts of time through the Claims Conference, which has led to some $60 billion from the German Government, money from the Austrian Government, from Germany and Austrian industry, that has helped survivors. And I am so appreciative for all of that.

But that doesn't mean that because that is what has been done, that there isn't more that can be done to address needs today.

And I will say it with respect to ICHEIC, that $300 million to survivors, $100 million to social service agencies, and the incredible commitment by really dedicated people who care about survivors can't be overlooked. And I am grateful for it. But suggesting that, when there are still real needs, that it is acceptable for us to have a conversation with those insurance companies to figure out how those needs can be met doesn't blow up the entire ICHEIC process, doesn't call into question the effectiveness of so many who have worked so hard, who worked so hard to put that in place. It simply means that we have to acknowledge what is on the ground now. And that is that there are survivors who have real needs that have to be met.

So I know that there is a lot of money being spent on lobbyists, on lawyers, on PR professionals across all different groups, public, private. I understand that. But I would just ask that if we can figure out how to calculate the needs, not, as I said earlier, based on some formula of so many hours are permitted. Forget about what is permitted. What is needed in order to help our survivors live out their lives in dignity? There are communities in this country that have done it. And then they have gone out and they have raised the money in order to meet those needs. Why can't we do that overall? Why can't we figure out what the needs are, while respecting the work that has been done by so many for so long? This is not about indicting one group or another, one individual or another. I have respect—and I will say it one more time—I have enormous respect for all of the people who have worked so hard to put in place the programs that exist, the Claims Conference that has negotiated all this money, ICHEIC that has negotiated a lot of money. But the needs haven't been met.

I said before and I will say again, we remain willing to work with all of these groups to figure out how to make sure that these needs are met and to do it in a respectful way and ask only from those who can help us reach this goal to work with us, not against us, and to know that together there is an opportunity to do right by Mr. Rubin and by everyone here.

And in Eugenie's father's, in Ivar's memory, and in memory of all those survivors who have passed on before we had this opportunity to get this right, let's work together on their behalf, in their memory. And on behalf of Mr. Rubin and the survivor community that he and Ms. Firestone and Dr. Paris and Ms. Lieberman and the chair and I and members of this Congress care so deeply about. We can do that. And I just hope that we have the opportunity.

I yield back.

Ms. Ros-Lehtinen. Thank you very much.

Mr. Clawson is recognized.

Mr. Clawson. Thank you. And I want to recognize the ranking member, both from Florida, and both who are—neither one listening to me right now, but both I have a great respect for——

Mr. Vargas. I am listening.

Mr. Clawson. These are wonderful leaders. And I second everything that they have said here today. As I heard you talk, it brought chills on my spine. My own parents are in the autumn time of their lifetime. And, you know, you wonder what I would feel like if they were in your position. And I can't imagine that. So I want to say that I appreciate you coming and sharing personal histories, personal things.

Ms. Lieberman, I have spent a lifetime in manufacturing. Never imagined myself here. Would have loved to have met the giant that your father was. And I think that you pay him great honor by doing what you are doing here today.

I don't have the background that my colleagues do on these issues. This is my first time in this subcommittee. But I do think that there is no greater crime than genocide, and that the results of that go on forever. It is unmatched in barbarity. And, in addition to the lives lost, the day I hear about the looting, I heard about the looting across Europe, money and jewelry. And today we hear about looting via insurance policies.

So, with me, you have an ally. My position is that the U.S. should lead and that Germany should step up. And I agree with what you said, Mrs. Firestone, to get it right, we should take care of these folks until the very last breath. And I am in full agreement with the concept and the heartfelt sentiment of that comment. I think deliverance—and the Jewish story is one of deliverance—and I think deliverance is never complete without financial justice as well, because I think—if I hear you right, Dr. Paris—that can help lead more easily to emotional justice and emotional peace. So I am on your side 100 percent in anything I can do to help you in your cause. I stand ready and willing.

While I have the mike, I would like to say I am also concerned about anti-Semitism in general in our world, the safety of Israel. You know, Hamas, Hezbollah, Iran, Syria, these sorts of nations and organizations make me feel uncomfortable. So as long as I am in Congress, I will do everything I can to help you and your cause to recover what is rightfully yours, and also anything I can do to help with the defense of Israel. And I appreciate you all coming today and for your sacrifices. Thank you.

Ms. Ros-Lehtinen. Thank you, Mr. Clawson. We welcome you to our fight. Thank you.

Mr. Vargas is recognized.

Mr. Vargas. Thank you very much, Madam Chair.

I appreciate everything that was said today, especially the testimony of the witnesses. You know, if there is one group that deserves justice in this world, it is the Holocaust survivors and their children. And it really is hard for me to understand why Germany doesn't come forward and meet its obligation, and why we allow it to not meet its obligation, why we don't do more. It seems that there is something that we could do. And I would join my colleagues in saying that, you know, if Germany won't do what it should do, we should stand up and we should do it. And we should in fact meet the needs of the survivors. I can't think of a group of people more worthy of getting their needs met. And like you said, not only their needs, but have some joy, for heaven sakes. I was thinking, as you were talking about family members, I am one of 10 kids. And my mom is one of over 10, as is my father. And their families were gigantic. And we have these gigantic families. And you are right, you know, I rejoice in the history and all the people that are around me and around my children. You know, what a horrible thing it would be not to have that. I couldn't agree with you more.

What should we do? Mr. Rubin, I mean, you have heard some of the testimony here. Why doesn't the United States stand up, do what Germany should do? Why don't we charge them? Why don't we send them the tab? Why don't we do that?

And for anybody that would care to answer that.

Ms. Firestone. Are you sure you want the answer, Congressman?

Mr. Vargas. Yes, I do. I am new, too. I am new, too. I want the answer.

Ms. Firestone. In 2011, my mother sat where I am sitting and testified before the full House Foreign Affairs Committee. She also sat before the Senate Judiciary Committee. One of the main roadblocks that we have to the insurance legislation that we came pressing for was our own State Department. They put the kibosh on our ability to go and have our day in court.

We have some survivors who were actually young enough when they got out, including my own uncle, who was 14 during the Holocaust, got out of Auschwitz, came here, and turned around and went back to Korea and served in Korea. We have survivors who were actually in the military and serving their country because they loved this country and saw it as their salvation.

And now we have our own Government standing in the way. The executive branch, the Office of the President also, we have been told that our country has offered ''legal peace'' to the insurance companies and Germany in exchange for them putting together ICHEIC, I believe. But ICHEIC was woefully inefficient, closed its doors and patted itself on the back that what a great job it did. The Claims Conference does the same thing.

But in the early—I believe it was 1982, but please don't hold me to that exact date, but I know it was in the 1980s, when I saw the bylaws that changed their mandate to not providing only for the survivors, but now there was what we call the 80–20 split, where 20 percent would go to Holocaust education and restitution. Did we really need the Claims Conference to do that? Almost every Holocaust museum and monument in this country was built by the survivors, was started by the survivors as a place where to memorialize their families.

Dr. PARIS. Mr. Vargas?

Mr. VARGAS. Yes, Doctor.

Dr. PARIS. I would like to answer that question from a different viewpoint and that being the squeaky wheel viewpoint. I think you are looking at a very few select witnesses here and that most survivors do not advocate for themselves in any way. That is the majority of the survivors. And I think that goes back to when they came to Israel and when they came to this country, no one cared, nobody wanted to listen. And they themselves buried their memories and went on with their lives to rebuild new families. Many have been extremely successful financially and in many other ways, many, many children, et cetera. They are only now in their older age unburying those memories and can't protect themselves anymore because of their mental—they are not able to mentally. But they no longer have the strength and the ability to advocate for themselves. So I think that is a big part of the problem also.

Mr. VARGAS. Thank you.

Madam Chair, thank you. I know my time is up, but I would be willing to help in any way, because I do think that this is an incredible injustice. And I can't think of a worthier group.

Ms. ROS-LEHTINEN. Thank you so much.

And we have got a great bill that you can cosponsor.

Mr. VARGAS. Put me on.

Ms. ROS-LEHTINEN. Thank you, sir.

Mr. RUBIN. Can I say one more thing?

Ms. ROS-LEHTINEN. Yes, Mr. Rubin.

And then we will go to Mr. Connolly.

Mr. RUBIN. I have been saying this all my life. Nazi Germany created this problem. And we, Americans, and you people who have the power to keep reminding Germany, you are responsible for this. And time has come when the need is great. You created it, and you have got to do what you are supposed to do to take care of the Holocaust survivors who are in need. And no ifs and no buts. It is up to you people. You have the power. You have the strength. And just go after Germany that you must do this. I mean, you can't just sit back and watch people fading away in misery. That is not fair to us. We are good American citizens. We love this country. I was fortunate enough to come to this country. But, in the meantime, to suffer and to see that the needy survivors are being neglected.

They came up with $800 million last year to be spread out for 4 years, which is $200 million. That is peanuts. That is a drop in the bucket. That is an insult. And that is why I beg you people, you have the strength. Please, don't forsake us. It is enough that Germany destroyed us, my whole family, my parents. I was a young man—young man, I was 14, 15 years old. I lost my parents. I lost their love. I didn't grow up to have their love or the love I could give them. But now is the time already. The need is survivors. We are begging you, it is in your hands. You have the strength. Do it for us, please. Because, you know, there is no time. Time is of the essence already. This thing should have taken care of yesterday, not tomorrow. Again, I beg you.

And I hope—I am 86 years old. I testified so many times that I don't even know how many times. I can no longer do it. I came up from Florida. I had to ask my son to come with me because I am feeling physically that I am giving out. But I see—I am on the advisory committee of Palm Beach County—I see what is going on. I see the need there. I am constantly in touch with the social workers. And they keep telling me, Jack, these people need 8 hours and some need 24 hours care, but we don't have the money. We don't have the money. And the money can only come from the German Government and insurance companies. So please do it. Do it for us.

Ms. ROS-LEHTINEN. Thank you very much, Mr. Rubin.

Pleased to yield to Mr. Connolly.

Mr. CONNOLLY. Thank you, Madam Chairman.

And thank you, Mr. Rubin, for that impassioned plea.

I was struck by all of your testimony, but particularly yours, Dr. Paris. I was so struck by the catalogue of afflictions. And part of the problem with, say, narrative coverage of the Holocaust as a point in history is survivors—you know, there were survivors. And I guess they all lived happily ever after. Almost no one talks about the lingering effects health-wise, and emotional, and psychological. Mr. Rubin just articulated it. He lost the love of parents as a young teenage boy. There is no getting that back.

I would be interested in just hearing a little bit more about the progression. Is it common that, say, to—to be able to function, a lot of memories and emotions are suppressed, but as one ages, they—they are revisited, whether we wish it or not? Would that be a fairly common phenomenon?

Ms. PARIS. Yes. Very common.

Mr. CONNOLLY. Could you please turn on your mic.

Ms. PARIS. I am sorry.

Mr. CONNOLLY. That is all right.

Ms. PARIS. Yes. Mr. Connolly, that is very, very common. As one has—as a young, healthy person—fairly healthy person, you have the ability to suppress memories and events and go on with your life and you are very busy raising. You are a family, trying to re-build your——

Mr. CONNOLLY. It is almost a necessary skill.

Ms. PARIS. It is totally necessary.

Mr. CONNOLLY. Otherwise, you are not going to be functional. Yeah.

Ms. PARIS. And society enforced that upon the survivors. Be-cause, if you listen, no one wanted to hear anything, no one wanted to believe anything, and they didn't even have an ear.

And they—you know, they wanted to integrate back into society, not be once again the outsiders, the people they were pointing fin-gers at as bad people or wrong people.

They wanted to be part of society, part of America. You have heard that today. They wanted not to be separated out anymore and singled out as Jews, even.

So I think—but when you get older and when your cognitive abilities are diminishing and you have plenty of time on your hands, it becomes much more difficult for your brain to suppress those memories.

And patients who become demented or have any cognitive im-pairment, they become disinhibited, which is a medical term, meaning they just can't suppress them anymore, medically speak-ing, and the horrors get relived.

As I pointed out in my opening comment, the patient was de-mented, but extremely hypervigilant. She—you know, "You are here, Dr. Paris," you know, and she didn't even know what world she was in. But she knew that I was there. Because she was afraid of a stranger in her house stealing something.

And then she would say, "I can't close my eyes. I can't close my eyes. I am in Auschwitz when I do that." And then she would start with the whole story of being a teenager there, having her head shaved, and it was horrible to listen to every time I went to visit her. And she didn't know she was telling me that. She never told me that when she was healthier.

Mr. CONNOLLY. You know, especially with dementia, the bound-aries between today and yesterday are very blurred. It is a very common phenomenon that dementia patients identify people who are deceased as very much alive and part of their world. So that doesn't surprise me at all, that that distinction between the past and the present kind of evaporates.

Has—is there assistance of any kind available formally for folks as they get older—survivors as they get older to try to help provide treatment and care for the psychological and physical conditions you were describing?

Ms. PARIS. I find it very challenging and difficult, as you pointed out, Mr. Rubin, to get any help.

I have many patients who are confused and demented, and they don't have 24-hour home care. They are living in unsafe situations.

They are possibly above the poverty line. So, they don't even qualify for Medicaid services, home attendance or a nursing home, not that they should, God forbid, go to a nursing home. I don't think that is the best place for them. And they just are alone in very dangerous situations.

And, you know, self-help gives, you know, 8 hours and this one gives 2 hours. And I can't even piece that together for them to get 24 hours. It is insane.

Mr. CONNOLLY. Thank you.

Ms. ROS-LEHTINEN. Thank you, Mr. Connolly.

I want to thank the witnesses for the courage, the stamina to once again come back up here and plead for justice.

We will do everything within our power to continue the fight, and we don't want to hear from the second generation, who are still coming up here and saying, "My father was not made whole, but I am here to fight for him." We want to make this generation whole, and we will continue that fight.

So we thank each and every one of you.

Mr. Rubin, I know that you are tired, but you can't give up. We need you. Thank you very much.

And, with that, the subcommittee hearing is adjourned. Thank you.

[Whereupon, at 4:51 p.m., the subcommittee was adjourned.]

APPENDIX

MATERIAL SUBMITTED FOR THE RECORD

JOINT SUBCOMMITTEE HEARING NOTICE
COMMITTEE ON FOREIGN AFFAIRS
U.S. HOUSE OF REPRESENTATIVES
WASHINGTON, DC 20515-6128

**Subcommittee on the Middle East and North Africa
Ileana Ros-Lehtinen (R-FL), Chairman**

**Subcommittee on Europe, Eurasia, and Emerging Threats
Dana Rohrabacher (R-CA), Chairman**

September 16, 2014

TO: MEMBERS OF THE COMMITTEE ON FOREIGN AFFAIRS

You are respectfully requested to attend an OPEN hearing of the Committee on Foreign Affairs, to be held jointly by the Subcommittee on the Middle East and North Africa and the Subcommittee on Europe, Eurasia, and Emerging Threats in Room 2172 of the Rayburn House Office Building (and available live on the Committee website at www.foreignaffairs.house.gov):

DATE: Thursday September 18, 2014

TIME: 3:00 p.m.

SUBJECT: The Struggles of Recovering Assets for Holocaust Survivors

WITNESSES: Mr. Jack Rubin
                 (Holocaust Survivor)

                 Ms. Klara Firestone
                 (Daughter of Holocaust Survivors)

                 Barbara Paris, M.D.
                 (Physician who focuses on the care of Holocaust Survivors)

                 Ms. Eugenie Lieberman
                 (Daughter of Holocaust Survivor)

By Direction of the Chairman

The Committee on Foreign Affairs seeks to make its facilities accessible to persons with disabilities. If you are in need of special accommodations, please call 202/225-5021 at least four business days in advance of the event, whenever practicable. Questions with regard to special accommodations in general (including availability of Committee materials in alternative formats and assistive listening devices) may be directed to the Committee.

COMMITTEE ON FOREIGN AFFAIRS

MINUTES OF SUBCOMMITTEE ON *Middle East and North Africa and Europe, Eurasia and Emerging Threats* HEARING

Day___*Thursday*___Date___*18 September 2014*___Room_____*2172*_____

Starting Time___*3:05 p.m.*___Ending Time___*4:51 p.m.*___

Recesses ___*0*___ (____to____)(____to____)(____to____)(____to____)(____to____)(____to____)

Presiding Member(s)

Chairman Ros-Lehtinen

Check all of the following that apply:

Open Session ✓
Executive (closed) Session ☐
Televised ✓

Electronically Recorded (taped) ✓
Stenographic Record ✓

TITLE OF HEARING:

The Struggles of Recovering Assets for Holocaust Survivors

SUBCOMMITTEE MEMBERS PRESENT:

Chairman Ros-Lehtinen, Chairman Rohrabacher, Reps. Chabot, Clawson, and DeSantis. Ranking Member Deutch, Ranking Member Keating, Reps. Ciciline, Vargas, and Schneider.

NON-SUBCOMMITTEE MEMBERS PRESENT: *(Mark with an * if they are not members of full committee.)*

HEARING WITNESSES: Same as meeting notice attached? Yes ✓ No ☐
(If "no", please list below and include title, agency, department, or organization.)

STATEMENTS FOR THE RECORD: *(List any statements submitted for the record.)*

SFR - Rep Connolly

TIME SCHEDULED TO RECONVENE_____
or
TIME ADJOURNED___*4:51 p.m.*___

Subcommittee Staff Director

STATEMENT OF KLARA FIRESTONE

UNITED STATES HOUSE OF REPRESENTATIVES

COMMITTEE ON FOREIGN AFFAIRS

The Struggles of Recovering Assets for Holocaust Survivors

September 18, 2014

My name is Klara Firestone. I was born in Prague, Czechoslovakia immediately following the end of World War II, and I am the daughter of two Holocaust survivors. I am the founder and president (for my second term) of Second Generation of Los Angeles, a founding member of Generations of the Shoah International (GSI), and sit on the Board of the Los Angeles Museum of the Holocaust, the first museum and monument to the Holocaust in the United States. Since founding Second Generation in 1978, I have been steeped in Holocaust affairs and have worked hand-in-glove with the members of the survivor community in Los Angeles and our surrounding counties. I come here today to speak on behalf of myself, my family, and the hundreds of Survivors and Second Generation who I have counseled and ministered to over the past 37years, and who have not had a voice to advocate for their rights. As the leader of Second Generation of Los Angeles, I have facilitated hundreds of support groups for children of Holocaust survivors, and in more recent years, after becoming a psychotherapist, I facilitated therapy groups for Second Generation. I have also been instrumental in helping survivor families navigate what have often been very complex and difficult relationships between parents and children given the extreme trauma that served as the backdrop for our developmental years, and most of our lives.

There is a long trail of problems that tens of thousands of survivors and family members have confronted, too often with incredibly frustrating and painful outcomes. The status quo is obviously not acceptable. If half of all survivors worldwide — including in the United States — are living today in or near poverty, unable to afford even the basics for a dignified old age, the approach of the past 50 years is obviously wrong. The temptation is great to dwell on the past, but we know you called this hearing to see what can be done TODAY to make a change for the better. What can be done today for survivors and their family members who have suffered terribly and continue to suffer? The answer is very plain:

Germany must assume the responsibility to provide for all medically necessary and basic income needs of all Survivors.

I would add my voice to the others who have discussed many of the medical and emotional issues that survivors and the Second Generation must deal with on a daily basis. The problems are real, and they require serious professional attention, with properly trained health care and psychological care givers who understand the unique problems that survivors and their children must deal with. Proper care requires a sea change in the funding available, and it is only just and right that this responsibility be assumed by the German government, and other entities that collaborated and profited from the Holocaust. Later in this statement, I address the extremely important issue of the plight and suffering of so many of our Second Generation members, who are the forgotten victims of the Nazi's atrocities and also deserve immediate and comprehensive support from Germany.

If this Committee does one thing as a result of this hearing, we ask that you undertake a concerted, bi-partisan, and relentless effort to convince Chancellor Merkel and the German Bundestadt to make good on Chancellor Adenauer's pledge in 1952 to take care of Holocaust survivors "to their last breath."

As my fellow panelist, Holocaust Survivor, Jack Rubin, stated in his OpEd response to this article, "But the fact is, Germany caused the massive medical and emotional problems survivors are confronting today, and Germany should pay for all of the survivors' needs, without the bargaining and compromising that has become the Claims Conference's specialty. Survivors and heirs should have the right to recover their lost assets, including German properties, insurance claims, and artworks, and Germany should pay for the needs of indigent survivors."

My testimony follows in the footsteps of my mother, Renee Firestone, who appeared before the full House Committee on Foreign Affairs on November 16, 2011, and before the Senate's Judiciary Committee on June 20, 2012. In the interest of conserving time, I have included her full written testimony to the House Committee as an exhibit to my written testimony and I reference it here, at this juncture. I wish, however, to point up a few salient points from her testimony.

At the age of 20, my mother was imprisoned for 13 months in the infamous death camp known as Auschwitz/Birkenau during the last years of World War II. Her mother, my grandmother, was never even processed into the camp, but was gassed immediately on arrival to Auschwitz. Six months after arrival at the camp, her 16 year old sister, after whom I am named , was first experimented upon before being shot by the Nazis to avoid her re-entering the general population of the camp and possibly exposing what the Nazis were doing. Her father, Morris, died of tuberculosis shortly after liberation. Her brother Frank, who had been a partisan . . . a resistance fighter . . . was the only other member of her immediate family to survive. In addition, we lost almost all of our huge extended family.

Following liberation in 1945, she was reunited with her brother and soon-to-be husband, my father Bernard, who had been in a Hungarian forced labor camp and then interned at Mauthausen concentration camp.

When the Holocaust ended, the fragments of Europe's Jewish communities emerged broken and tattered, wanting nothing more than to find who of their families survived and begin rebuilding their lives. They were too busy fighting their "demons" to care about fighting bureaucracy in order to claim what was due them. Many believed, as my mother also did then, that this was "blood money" and wanted nothing to do with it. They asked the question, "How can you compensate me for the loss of my parents, brothers, sisters, aunts, uncles, cousins, etc. in dollars? What value should I assign that? So once again, their claims and needs went unmet. In the years immediately after the war, these very young survivors traveled to whichever country would allow them access and safe haven, thankful to have the chance at new lives. A handful made it to phenomenal wealth, but the majority did not, and today the educated estimates are that approximately half of all survivors in the United States are living at or below the poverty line. Yet when they have tried in the past to gain some measure of justice, they have been met with the appalling intransigence of the Claims Conference leadership and had the doors slammed in their faces.

Can someone please tell me why, after suffering the humiliations and brutality of the Nazis, the survivors must now go begging for what is rightfully due them, suffering additional indignities and being re-traumatized, only this time by the ones who are ostensibly there to aid them! If you could hear the comments and cries of the survivors at this betrayal, it would break your hearts, just as it broke mine.

As the most active and visible leaders in our survivor community, my mother and I have been approached hundreds of times by survivors and their children beseeching us to intervene on their behalf to recover restitution which is rightfully theirs. Time and time again we have attempted to do just that, and we, too, have been unsuccessful.

Even advocating for my own family has proved to no avail. My beloved father passed away in 2001. Prior to his death, he had received a letter from the Claims Conference confirming that they had assigned him a claim number for a particular fund and he would soon be receiving the monies. After contacting them numerous times over the years, we are still waiting for those funds. They now claim that they are unable to find his claim in the system. You cannot imagine the pain this causes the loved ones of a Holocaust survivor, not to mention re-traumatizing the survivors themselves, and this is the kind of problem I hear about over and over again.

With so many obstacles to obtaining what belonged to them, the survivors sought a different route to recover some part of their family legacies. They attempted to file claims with the insurance companies that had insured their parents' lives and properties through the auspices of ICHEIC, the International Committee on Holocaust Era Insurance Claims. Once again they hit a wall, thwarted by the ineffectiveness of ICHEIC.

My mother spoke to me numerous times about her certainty that her father had insurance to cover his business, their home, and his life. Her comment was almost always the same, "My father was sort of the patriarch of the family. Everyone, including his brothers and sisters would come to him for advice on all matters. Why would he advise his relatives to get insurance and then not purchase it for himself and his family?" This makes no logical sense. By a stroke of magical luck, my mother's first cousin found some documents when he went home after the war, including the insurance policy of his parents. He was the very first survivor to recover from ICHEIC because of this document, although others were not so lucky. And when the children of his deceased brothers finally discovered that they could claim as well, they tried but were told that the claim had already been paid. So much for "adequate and sufficient notice to claimants."

As my mother stated in her testimony on November 16, 2011,

> *My father was a very responsible man, with a business and real property in order to provide our family with an upper middle class standard of living in pre-war Czechoslovakia (annexed by Hungary in 1938). I am certain he had insurance. But when I filed my claim, after all the fanfare, the Commission (ICHEIC) informed me that his name was not on any of the lists. This is difficult for me to accept, but since it is well-known that the lists produced by Generali and the other insurance companies were incomplete, I wonder why the U.S.*

government has neither demanded a full accounting, nor allowed the states to require it.

* * *

Here are some facts that this Committee and Congress should know about when they come to evaluate the insurance companies' and anyone else's claim that Holocaust survivors, and the children and grandchildren of Holocaust victims, should be satisfied with ICHEIC, rather than have our rights enforced.

ICHEIC was chartered under Swiss law and headquartered in London to avoid American public record laws and court subpoenas. It was funded by the insurance companies themselves, its meetings were conducted in secret, and minutes were not even published of the secret meetings.

Almost all survivors were frustrated and insulted by their ICHEIC experiences. This was conveyed to Congress in a series of hearings between 2000 and 2003. The survivors regaled experiences such as multi-year waits for responses, denials without any explanation, demands for information that no claimant could be expected to know (such as the birthdates or death certificates of relatives who perished in the Holocaust), and denials of claims even where policies were proven to have existed (Generali's "Negative Evidence Rule").

In its first five years, **ICHEIC spent more money on administrative expenses than it paid in claims**. Chairman Lawrence Eagleburger told a Congressional Committee that ICHEIC's internal processes were "none of its [Congress's] business."

In 2002, Congressman Henry Waxman wrote: "Holocaust survivors have been waiting decades to reclaim Holocaust-era insurance policies. Unfortunately, the . . . majority of the companies that have agreed to the ICHEIC process have not lived up to their obligation to disclose policyholder lists. The ICHEIC member companies also appear to have wrongfully rejected, undervalued or left unanswered the claims of many survivors."

In 2003, Congress even passed a law -- the Foreign Affairs Authorization Act -- that required the State Department to collect information on ICHEIC companies' claims, practices, and results. However, **ICHEIC refused to comply with this requirement** as the State Department reported in its annual reports each year.

When ICHEIC ended in 2007, it had paid fewer than 14,000 of the 800,000 life/annuity/endowment polices estimated to be owned by European Jews in 1938. The total paid on policies was $250 million, less than three percent (3%) of the $18 billion in outstanding values at the time, according to the estimate of economist Zabludoff, using what he regards as very conservative numbers. Today the unpaid amount of Holocaust era insurance policies exceeds $20 billion.

ICHEIC also issued 34,000 checks for $1000 each which it termed "humanitarian" in nature, but which survivors considered insulting rejections. Yet ICHEIC and its supporters today take credit for having "paid 48,000 claims," an obvious attempt to inflate its results and give the appearance of success to a process that badly failed.

You can also imagine our shock when, after ICHEIC ended, its Chief Executive Officer, Mara Rudman, became a paid lobbyist for the American Insurance Association – the umbrella U.S. group lobbying against the original version of HR 890 that was introduced by the late Congressman Tom Lantos in 2007. Mr. Lantos, the only Holocaust survivor to ever serve in Congress, was a dear friend of mine. His widow, Annette Lantos, as well as his daughter Katrina, have remained committed advocates for the rights of Holocaust survivors.

As a Californian, I am also proud to say that our Insurance Commissioners, especially former Commissioner, and now Congressman, John Garamendi, were among the very few who stood toe to toe with the insurance companies and even the Jewish groups on ICHEIC who were so ready to cave into the insurance companies and short-change the survivors. Mr. Garamendi fought passionately for our interests.

Unfortunately, despite Mr. Garamendi's tireless efforts to make ICHEIC work to benefit claimants, the insurance companies won big by paying so few policies, by paying such small settlements, and by convincing the Supreme Court that the states did not have the right to allow us Holocaust survivors to hold the insurers accountable for their actions. This loss was devastating, and shocked survivors throughout the State and the country.

Not only are we distraught over the way the courts have disrespected Holocaust survivors, but the records that the Holocaust Survivors Foundation USA has found under the Freedom of Information Act show that the State and Justice Departments acted terribly in their court papers and Congressional testimony. We cannot understand how our own government became the adversary of Holocaust survivors in the 21st Century.

Despite the claim that the United States and Europe have been "successful in Holocaust restitution," that is far from the truth. Specific property restitution for individuals has been largely unfulfilled. Only a fraction of the properties actually looted during the Holocaust were "recovered" or restituted in any general sense, and of those funds, only a small portion recovered and deemed "heirless" or for "humanitarian purposes" has trickled down to meet the pressing social service needs of the remaining Holocaust survivors.

Tragically, tens of thousands of survivors, including many thousands in the US, are facing dire problems. They cannot meet basic home and health care needs, or pay for medicines, dentures, eyeglasses, hearing aids, or walkers, or receive transportation to the doctor. This may shock most leaders and public officials, but it has been documented with increasing frequency in the Jewish and mainstream media.

In the United States, half of all survivors   more than 50,000   either live below the poverty line (25%) or have incomes so low they are considered "poor" given the cost of living in their communities. In my hometown of Los Angeles, 39% of all Holocaust survivors live below the poverty line. This is a moral and human tragedy that should never have been accepted, but it was, and it continues today. Yet we survivors, and our children, are dealing with these tragedies day in and day out, and the governmental and philanthropic establishments have been sadly protective of status quo organizations and corporations, rather than protective of survivors' rights, interests, and needs.

How did this state of affairs come to pass? The role of the Conference on Jewish Material Claims Against Germany, Inc. ("Claims Conference") in the restitution failures is a common thread that cannot be ignored. One of the reasons victims have done so badly in the property and insurance negotiations is that the organizations primarily doing the negotiating (the Claims Conference, the World Jewish Congress, the World Jewish Restitution Organization—WJRO) are less interested in individual claims being honored than in "global settlements" which result in funds they can control. Even Stuart Eizenstat, no champion of survivors' rights, recognized this in his book Imperfect Justice.

As reported in the media and testified in Congressional committees, the Claims Conference has drawn the ire of Holocaust survivors throughout the world for its lack of survivor representation in policy making, for policies that cause grave harm to thousands of impoverished survivors, for its lack of transparency in the handling of restituted assets, and worst of all, for its use of restitution funds for pet projects including grants to board members and cronies of organization officials, and other serious concerns.

The Claims Conference is a creation of the early 1950's. It reflects a political decision made by leaders of the Jewish community and the German government, in the aftermath of the Holocaust, to have a mechanism to channel German reparations to Holocaust survivors. For over 40 years, there were no official survivor organizations on the Claims Conference board of directors. In the 1990's two "survivor groups" were added to the board, but today only 2 of the 24 voting board members are survivor organizations. So, the Claims Conference's board members and officers were neither elected by survivors, nor does it morally represent the Nazi victims in whose names the organization obtains its funds.

After German reunification in the early 90s, Germany passed a law making the Claims Conference the legal heir ("successor organization") to East German properties not claimed by direct heirs within the outrageously short time limit set by the Germans. However, the Conference did not publish information about the names of the Jewish owners of these properties, and then claimed them as their own! To make matters worse, the courts have supported the Claims Conference's claim to ownership of such properties – even against the legitimate heirs of Holocaust victims who had no idea about the two year deadline including many who understandably had no idea about family assets before the devastation of the Holocaust.

*Moreover, the Claims Conference has never fully accounted for nor disclosed information about properties it obtained after German reunification that were owned by Jews before World War II. Nor has there ever been an audit of the organization's asset base by an independent **outside** authority that is accountable to the public or the government.*

The shell game taking place was that the Claims Conference ousted thousands of German property heirs of their rights, and then turned around and used the properties for various "research, documentation, and education" projects which were only authorized for the Claims Conference after it amended its by-laws in 1994 – not coincidentally after becoming the "owner" of the "heirless" Jewish German properties.

Yet, without a mandate to use all of the funds at its disposal for the needs of survivors, it has spent far in excess of $250 million in the last 15 years on projects unrelated to survivors and their welfare. Many of these "research, documentation, and education grants are made to organizations that sit on the Claims Conference Board of Directors. Survivors question the legitimacy of these grants, and have for over a decade, yet we hear silence from most public officials and private community leaders.

Let me repeat – despite tens of thousands of impoverished Holocaust survivors suffering from inadequate nutrition, housing, medical care, home care, and other vital services, the Claims Conference has seen fit to squander $250 million for non-survivor "research, education and documentation" projects, including many insider grants – a quarter of a billion dollars worth of guaranteed Holocaust survivor suffering intentionally imposed by the Claims Conference. How can Congress and other leaders be silent in the face of such cruelty?

There has never been a full, public accounting of the actual value of the assets, including real estate, art, and other properties in the Claims Conference's inventory of assets. This lack of information is not only inconsistent with all modern notions of necessary transparency of organizations dealing with the public trust, but it makes a mockery of the constant refrain of the past decade -- that it "does not have enough funds" to meet the current needs of survivors around the world.

Among the many terrible, painful, and disgraceful indignities we have been made to suffer occurred in 2002 when Israel Singer, then-President of the Claims Conference (and simultaneously Secretary General of the World Jewish Congress) wrote an article in a prominent Jewish journal giving elaborate details about all of the education and building projects that the Claims Conference was going to create "**with Holocaust restitution funds after the survivors are gone.**" *This column outraged survivors throughout the country, as Holocaust Survivors Foundation USA President David Schaecter wrote in response:*

How can plans for a "Jewish People's Fund" go forward while survivors languish on waiting lists for the health care they deserve, especially after all they have endured? How dare these institutions presume to spend "restituted" funds for their favored "philanthropic" projects into the next century, using money claimed from the most terrorized victims of the past century? Who will take responsibility for ensuring that the individuals around whom much of our modern

*Jewish existence is centered - Holocaust victims - are not abandoned
a second time?*

*Despite an outpouring of survivor anger, and limited media coverage of this
startling admission by Rabbi Singer that what the survivors had feared all along
was really being planned, very little changed. Pressure from some communities
has caused the Claims Conference to increase allocations here, and there, as if
they were applying grease to a squeaky wheel.   But how can survivors' rights be
toyed with so shamelessly?*

*You might recognize Mr. Singer's name.   He was dismissed in early 2007
from his position as Secretary General of the World Jewish Congress for a variety
of financial improprieties, including taking over a million dollars from one of the
Claims Conference organizations (the Jewish Agency) and placing it in a secret
Swiss Bank account.   Yet for a long period, he retained his position as President
of the Claims Conference, while the Chairman, Julius Berman (who remains
Chairman today), saw "no reason to take action" and remove him because Rabbi
Singer allegedly "has never been involved in the financial decisions of the Claims
Conference." Ultimately, public pressure caused the Claims Conference to
dismiss Rabbi Singer.*

*However, for purposes of HR 890, it is important for this Committee to
understand that during the entire ICHEIC period, when it opened in 1998 until it
closed in March 2007, Israel Singer was the "leading" voice of the "Jewish" side.
As noted, this was a body where the insurance companies were fully represented,
but not claimants. ICHEIC documents show that Rabbi Singer himself
represented three different "Jewish groups" on ICHEIC – the Claims Conference,
the World Jewish Congress, and the World Jewish Restitution Organization
(WJRO).   So, when these groups stand before Congress to oppose my
constitutional right as an American citizen to go to court against these insurers,
based on ICHEIC, they are really defending outcomes engineered or approved by
an insular group of non-elected and non-representative big-shots with no legal or
moral right to speak or act for us, the victims, or our families.*

*The Claims Conference has continued to act as if it owns these survivor
funds, and the sincere outcry of decent people has been overwhelmed by the
institutional power of the Claims Conference's funding practices.   These practices
include silencing opposition by funding a myriad of non-survivor programs around
the world, and by creating the fear in communities that it might reduce the minimal
funding it provides to Jewish family service organizations for survivors' needs.*

Had they been able to pursue a recovery on these insurance policies, perhaps we would not have had the need to be here today and the survivors would have had the financial resources to live out their golden years in peaceful and dignified security.

In more recent years, the Survivors trusted that the U.S. government believed the survivors had made great contributions to their adopted homeland and were valuable enough to accord them the same rights as every other citizen of this great country. And here, too, they were grossly disappointed . . . by our own State Department, Executive Branch of our government, and by Congress in not restoring the survivors' right to have their "day in court" against the insurance companies.

Finally, I wish to touch on an issue which has yet to be discussed, but vitally important, and which has no other platform to be heard. And that is the plight and suffering of many of our Second Generation members. Although we are not always certain of the mechanism and how it functions, there is an awareness now of something called "transmitted trauma," the concept that the trauma our parents went through has been passed down to some of us, the results of which manifest as if they themselves had experienced the trauma directly. They exhibit a sort of vicarious PTSD, Post-Traumatic Stress Disorder, with all the attendant symptomology . . . "flashbacks" of events that they did not experience, but were most likely gained from stories fed to them "with mother's milk" at an impressionable age, irrational fears such as people coming in the middle of the night to take them away, hallucinations that Nazi soldiers are coming down the aisles in a movie theater, startle reflex, etc. I can't begin to tell you the number of desperate calls I have received from survivor parents troubled over their child's mental health. Some of these children have been so damaged by the time they reached their teenage years that they have been totally disabled and dysfunctional for the rest of their lives. Additionally, for some of them who have only been marginally affected by their parents' experiences, the stresses of now having to be caregivers to their parents while experiencing financial hardships has taken an enormous emotional toll on us. The survivors come with unique "baggage" that only serves to exacerbate the already difficult and stressful task of caring for an aging parent.

We have watched and suffered alongside our parents in their struggle for justice. The thought that our "inheritance" will go into the coffers of the Claims Conference and its affiliates just heightens our frustration and pain. On June 22, 2014, the JTA published an article entitled *Considering future, Claims Conference weighs shutting down vs. Holocaust Education.* In that article, the Claims Conference stated, "Given the Claims Conference's successes at convincing Germany to increase its funding for survivors, the panel concluded that "to close down without attempting to leverage its position and significant experience in the service of Holocaust education and remembrance would be to miss a major opportunity."http://www.jewishpress.com/news/breaking-news/considering-future-claims-conference-weighs-shutting-down-vs-holocaust-education/2014/06/22/." The survivor community's response was incredulous. First, with half of all survivors living in or near the poverty line and lacking the funds they need for even basic necessities of life, the statement that the Claims Conference has been "successful" in obtaining funding for survivors defies reality.

Further, it is offensive to survivors and their family members to perpetrate the myth that the Claims Conference is indispensable for Holocaust education and remembrance. Who do they think has been providing it all these years since the end of the Holocaust? The answer is: The Holocaust Survivors and their families. Who has spearheaded and funded all the Holocaust museums and memorials and monuments in this country and abroad? The survivors! And who began the process of educating the masses on the atrocities and lessons gleaned from the Holocaust? The Survivors! My mother said to me, "If they want to pay for Holocaust education, they can start by paying me for the 35 years I have been speaking to the world about my experiences."

And, in the unlikely event that any funds should remain after the last of the Survivors have left this world, those funds are the rightful inheritance of the children and grandchildren of the Survivors, and only they can and should decide how that is disposed of.

We children of survivors feel the inadequacy of our words whenever we attempt to convey the suffering of our parents and families to others, especially to the members of this Honorable Committee, our own representatives, all of which suffering was for no good reason. Except now, we have the platform to express the harsh fact that Germany has shirked its responsibilities to our loved ones who are without adequate resources to be cared for properly and to allow for a healing of the physical and mental wounds obtained at the hands the Nazi German Regime. Why should others who are not the perpetrators be pushed to provide inadequate resources thus allowing the tragic suffering to continue to this day without relief?

That is why we are so grateful to you, the members of this Committee, for the opportunity to plead our cause and to urge you, in the strongest terms, to use your power and press our own government, starting with the President, the Secretary of State and the Attorney General, and all of you, to demand that Germany provide the ADEQUATE funds necessary until all survivors have gone, as was promised by Chancellor Adenauer right after the War's end. Our efforts for decades in this regard were without appropriate answers. Nothing! Instead silence. followed by crumbs when the funders got around to it.

It is "one minute to Midnight" and if something is not done quickly and sufficiently, my fear is that thousands of the remaining survivors will die tragically, suffering their unmet medical and psychological needs.

Simply put, Germany must resume its moral responsibility to care for ALL the medical and mental health needs of the survivors and their families, with no more back turning or sloughing off these huge responsibilities onto the shoulders of others.

We call upon this honorable Committee and its members to press Chancellor Merkel and the German government to **fully** fund the needs of our aging Survivors, without offset or delay.

Chairman Ros-Lehtinen, thank you for allowing me to testify, and I request that I can submit the attached exhibits in the Hearing Record. I also wish to thank Chairman Royce for allowing Mr. Rohrabacher, Chairman of the Europe Subcommittee, and Ms. Ros-Lehtinen and Mr. Deutch, Chairman and Ranking Member of the Middle East and North Africa Subcommittee, to hold this hearing. I thank Mr. Rohrabacher for agreeing to co-sponsor this hearing. And, a most special thank you goes to Congresswoman Ros-Lehtinen and Congressman Ted Deutch, who have been the most steadfast supporters of the Survivor community and champions of our cause against tremendous odds, for many, many years.

Statement for the Record
Submitted by Mr. Connolly of Virginia

Today, we examine the challenges faced by Holocaust survivors in the United States as they age, seek access to services, and maintain the quality of life they deserve. The panel for this hearing includes a survivor, Jack Rubin. Mr. Rubin's presence is a stark reminder that the atrocities of the Holocaust were carried out not all that long ago.

It was in 20th century Europe that a brutal dictator murdered 6 million Jews, including 1 million children. As the Nazis advanced across Europe and gained territory, they expanded the system of concentration camps designed to systematically imprison and exterminate an entire population of people. At its height, the infrastructure of the Holocaust included over 40,000 facilities and hundreds of thousands of personnel.

It is important to highlight the size and scope of the Holocaust as well as its place in our recent history. In doing so, we are reminded that this was not an isolated incident and we cannot divorce the lessons of this tragedy from contemporary threats. Anti-Semitism, religious persecution, and genocide remain modern scourges that require our vigilance.

I am a cosponsor of H. Res. 707, condemning anti-Semitism and supporting efforts by the United States to combat this particularly insidious form of prejudice. The measure also supports U.S. initiatives that make the fight against anti-Semitism part of our foreign policy priorities. This includes the mandate for the United States Special Envoy to Monitor and Combat Anti-Semitism and support for Holocaust education initiatives abroad.

Mr. Rubin, I want to thank you for joining us today. Your participation in this hearing is so important for the reasons I have enumerated, but also we benefit from a first person perspective on the challenges facing the Holocaust survivor community. As the survivor community ages, new issues are arising. The well-documented fear of doctors many survivors experience compounds health problems which occur with greater frequency among seniors. The median age of survivors in the United States is 82, and there are as many as 130,000 survivors residing in the U.S. I mention these facts to illustrate that our survivors are aging, but still very much a presence in communities across the U.S.

Let me be clear. Nothing can make Holocaust survivors whole. Their experiences of Adolf Hitler's brand of evil and the pain and suffering it produced will be with them forever. However, our hearing today is about what we can do to meet their unique challenges and ensure that they do not lack the resources or services to live the life they fought so valiantly to protect against all odds. In a military and humanitarian campaign that tested the mettle of the West, we ultimately defeated the Nazis and their reign of terror. However, so long as survivors are with us, the mission is not complete.